CW01305526

THIS JOURNAL BELONGS TO

*O God, The Giver of Life,
Remover of pains and sorrows,
Bestower of happiness, and
Creator of the Universe;
Thou art luminous, pure and adorable;
We meditate on Thee;.
May Thou inspire and guide
Our intellect in the right direction.*
— Gayatri Mantra of Lord Ganesha

INTRODUCTION

The *Whispers of Lord Ganesha Journal* is designed to help you clear any creative blocks you feel are holding you back from progressing through the next steps in your life. Expressing your thoughts and emotions in these pages will help you process whatever is going on for you when you sit down to write. Your writing will serve as an outlet for your inner-most feelings and will help you discover your true desires and how you would like to achieve them.

Lord Ganesha is the elephant-headed deity of the Hindu pantheon. He is known to assist with the beginning of new projects and to remove obstacles that might show up in your path. Lord Ganesha gives knowledge to the seeker of wisdom, and prosperity to those who long for worldly gains. He supports families who want children and blesses individuals on the spiritual path with salvation.

To make a start in your new journal, you might like to write about where you feel you are at this point in your life. Write about where you live or work, the main relationships that influence your life and what intrigues you. Are you where you want to be? Questioning yourself will help you gain clarity as you embark on this journaling journey.

Consider writing from your stream of consciousness. To do this, set a timer for five or ten minutes, and just begin writing. Write anything and everything that comes to mind. Write nonstop, without correcting your grammar or censoring your thoughts and feelings. Allow yourself to write continuously and freely without judging the content.

Keep a list of things you appreciate. Count the many blessings in your life, whether they be things you value, or people you're grateful for, and write them all down. You can decide if you would like to have your appreciation list in a specific area of your journal or if you would like to have the blessings list sprinkled throughout your journal. Also consider including quotes that you find encouraging and inspirational.

In addition to listing your blessings, think about noting down your successes and the goals you have attained. Big successes might include promotions or a monumental day in your life. As you do this, try to take note of any small realizations you come to during your week. Heightened awareness of your accomplishments will encourage you and may even motivate you for a new triumph.

If you feel you are blocked by an experience you are obsessing over, try writing about it from another person's perspective, perhaps that of the person you are conflicted about. Sometimes, when you put yourself in another's position, you can gain new insights, and clear what had been hindering you.

Use your *Whispers of Lord Ganesha Journal* to let go of fears, blocks, restrictive beliefs and unhealthy habits. Your writing will also help you focus your energy on manifesting new dreams and becoming clearer about your purpose for your life. Meditate and record your emotions. See this as an opportunity to create for your future and shift the energy from your past. Sometimes journaling can help you to gain clarity, to change your mind, or to set a new, more fulfilling direction.

As you continue your journaling practice and nurture your connection with Lord Ganesha, may your love of self deepen and your confidence grow ever greater.

Namaste,

Angela Hartfield

At the start of every endeavor, you will find Lord Ganesha.

Ask Lord Ganesha to assist you with new energy for the opportunities ahead.

Never give up. Keep your thoughts and your mind always on the goal.
— Tom Bradley

One of the secrets of success is to refuse to let temporary setbacks defeat you.
— Mary Kay Ash

Lord Ganesha beckons you to retreat into a calm environment to replenish your energy and regain your composure.

Ganesha gently guides you to surrender this challenge for a while. Take some time for yourself.

It is better to strive in one's own dharma than to succeed in the dharma of another.
— The Ganesha Gita

Laughter is a gift. A little humor can give you an incredible energy boost.

Honor the wisdom within yourself.

Appreciate silence, and allow your inner light to shine out toward others as a means of communication.

*You have access to high levels of energy and movement that
propel you forward to achieve your goals.*

*In the movement of dance, Ganesha expresses emotion in a physical
way thus uniting the body with the spirit.*

Your root chakra is associated with keeping life exciting and sustainable. When the root chakra energy is in balance, you are centered, grounded, healthy, vibrant, and will have unlimited physical energy.

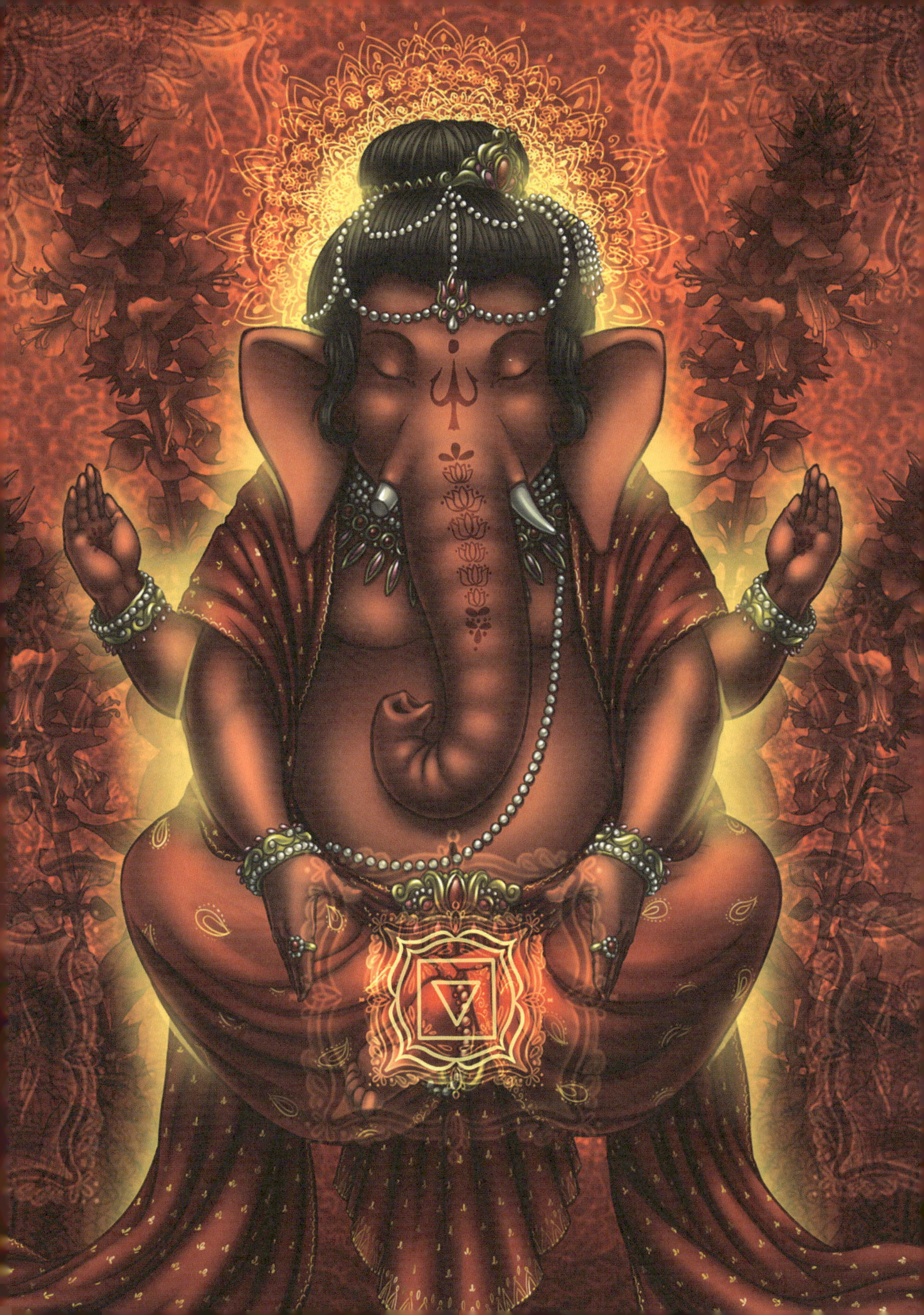

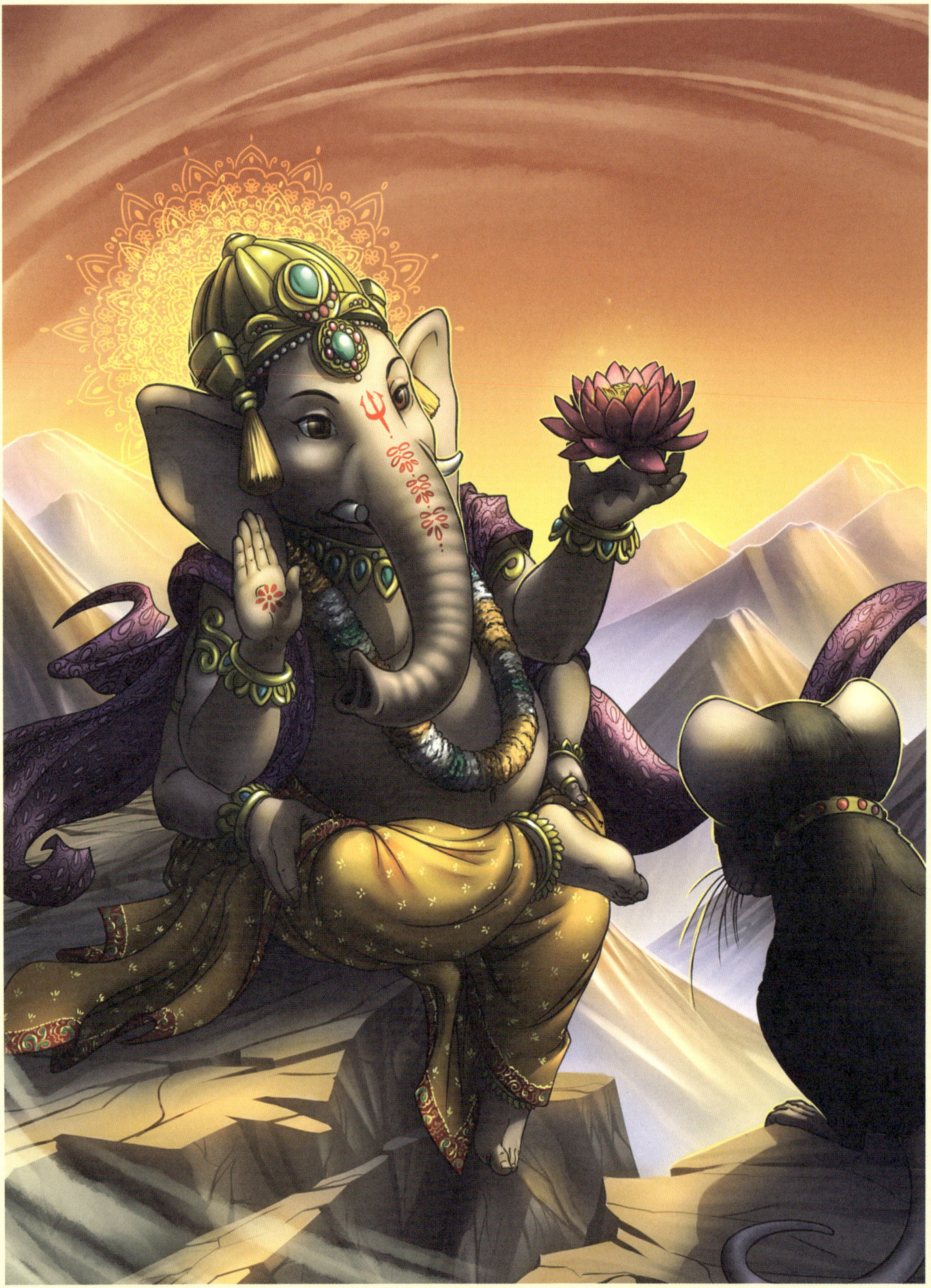

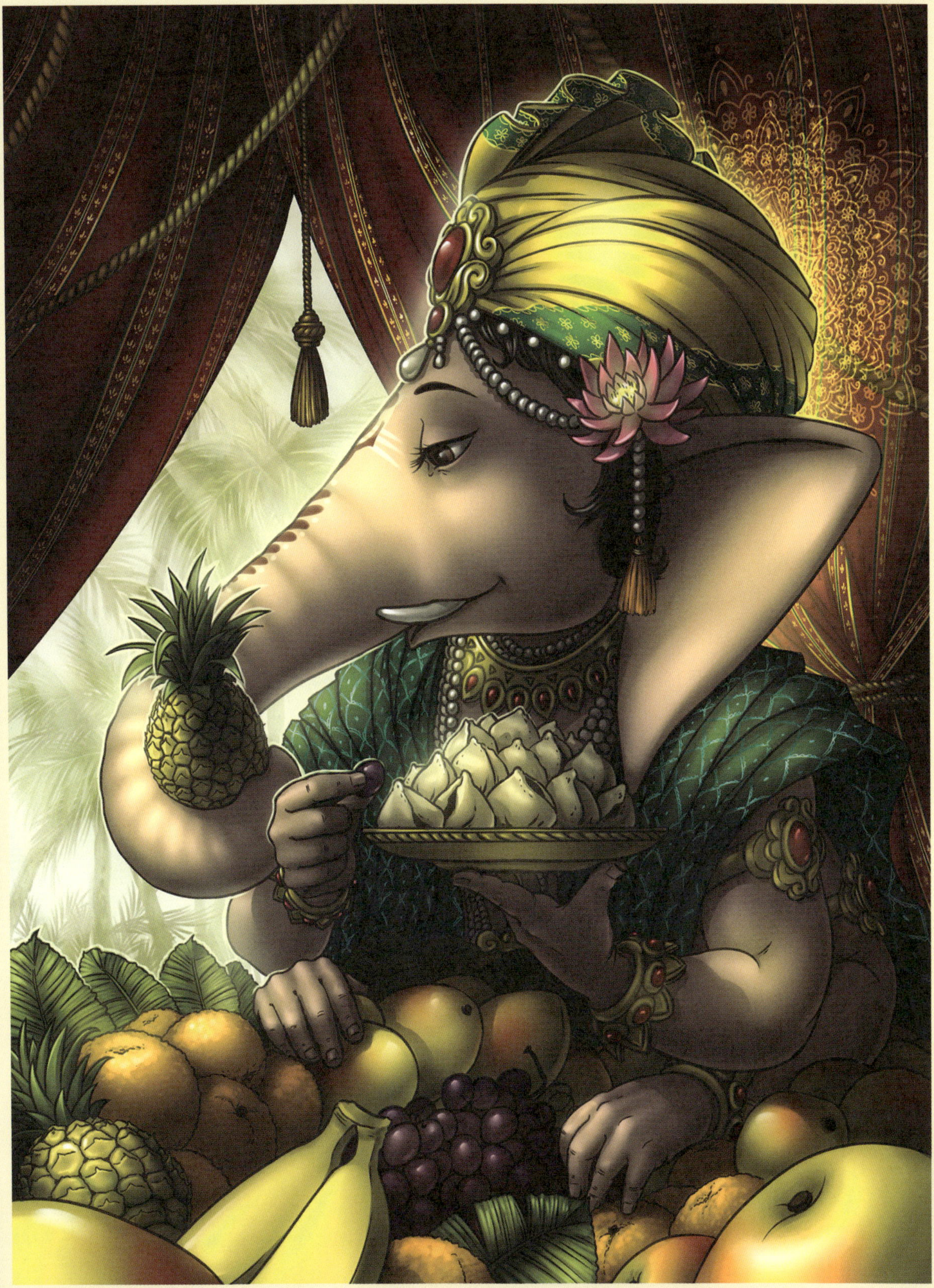

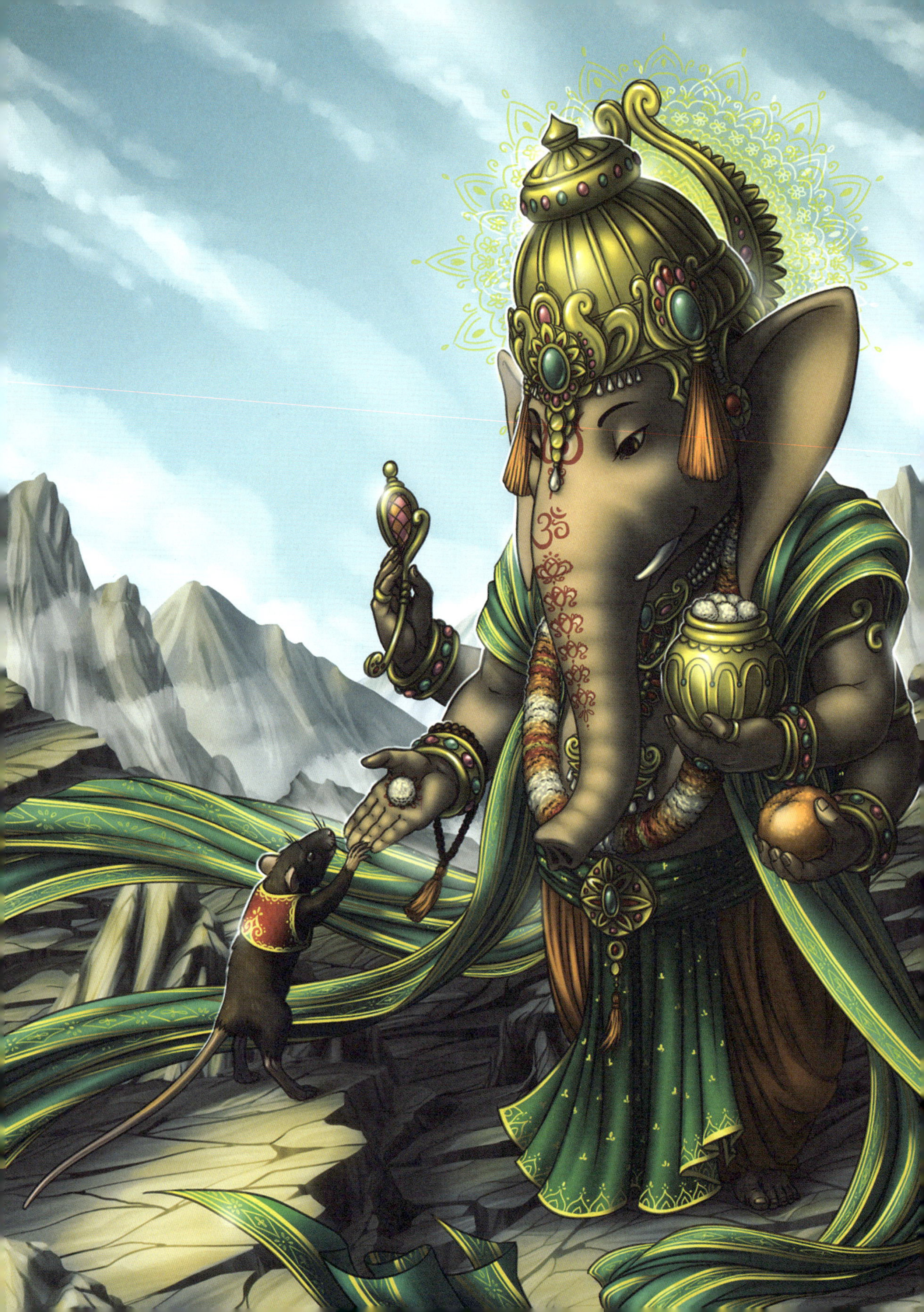

The first song that I wrote was when I was with The Del Rios. I was like 14 years old but I was always putting my thoughts down on paper even before then because it was like an escape - a way of unleashing all the stuff.
— William Bell

*No matter what you want to do or become,
you will achieve more with knowledge.*

*When wisdom is covered by anger and desire, it confuses the person
who would otherwise possess intuitive knowledge.*
— The Ganesha Gita

*When pictured reading the scroll, Ganesha reminds us of the
importance of education and the pursuit of knowledge.*

Ask Ganesha to help you lighten up through laughter.

Ganesha encourages you to appreciate all the blessings, treats, gifts, friendships and love that surround you.

*When you deny your need to create, experience, and grow,
it is to your own detriment.*

Only you can truly know what your soul desires.

Ganesha asks that you take time to reflect on your desires and dreams.

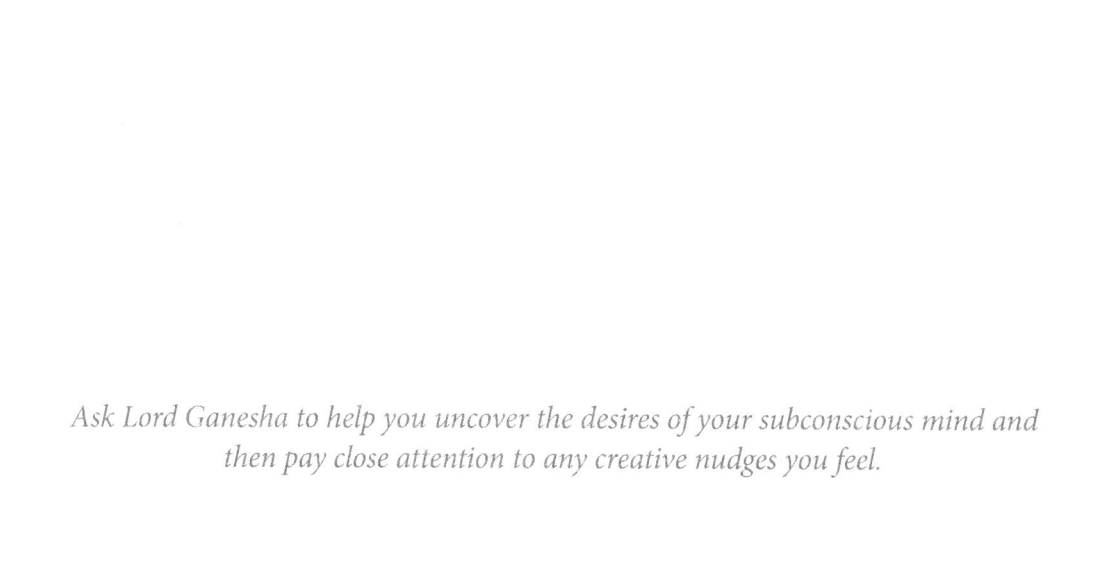

Ask Lord Ganesha to help you uncover the desires of your subconscious mind and then pay close attention to any creative nudges you feel.

Take time to acknowledge and understand your lessons and your blessings.

Reflect on your past endeavors, and be proud of how far you've come.

How would your life be different if... You walked away from gossip and verbal defamation? Let today be the day... You speak only the good you know of other people and encourage others to do the same.

— Steve Maraboli

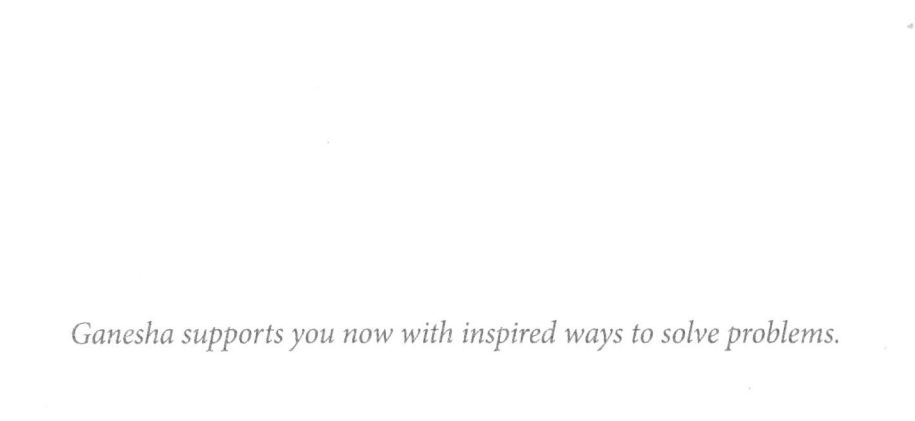

Ganesha supports you now with inspired ways to solve problems.

Commit to the task at hand, and eliminate distractions that take your attention away from your end goal.

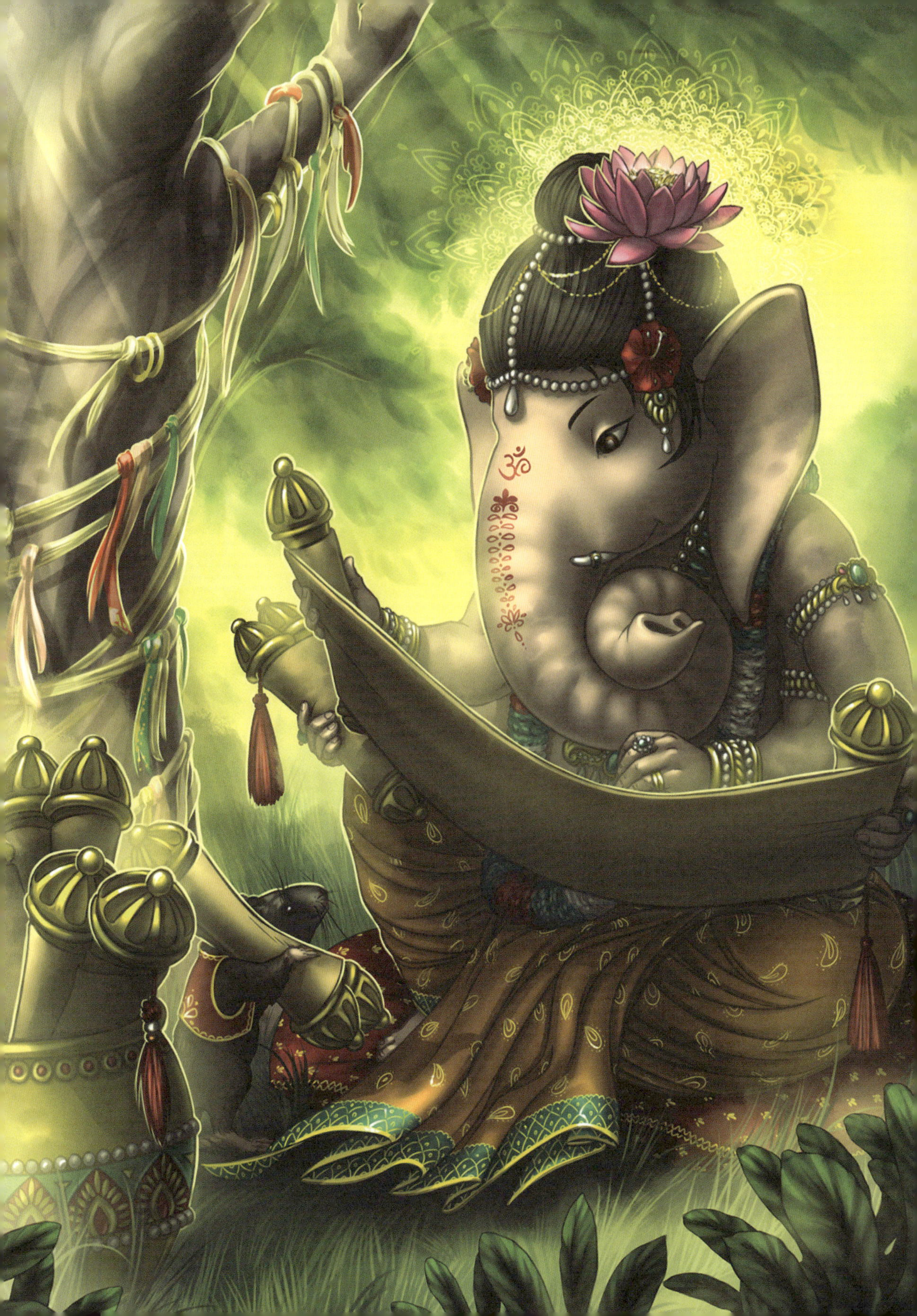

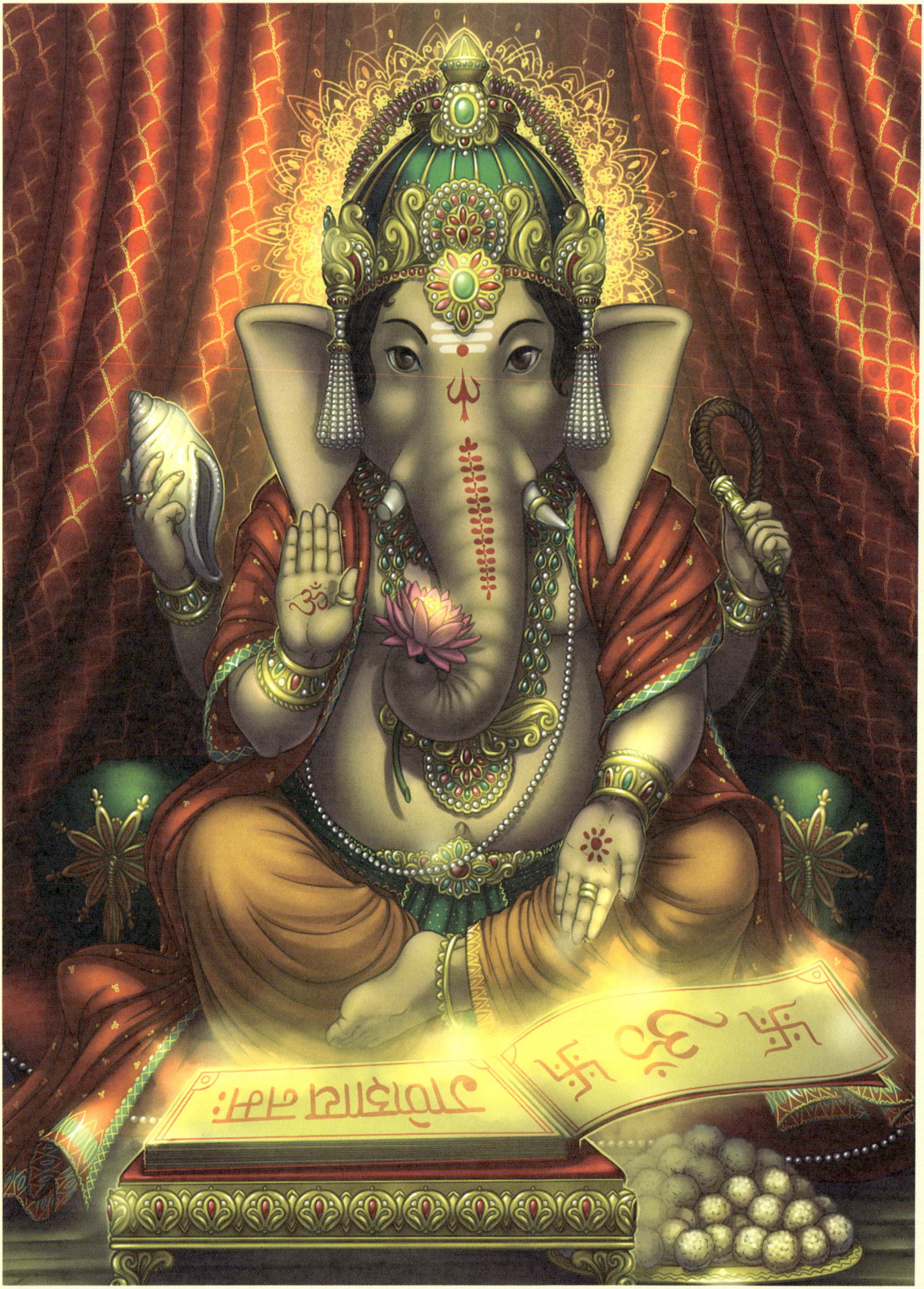

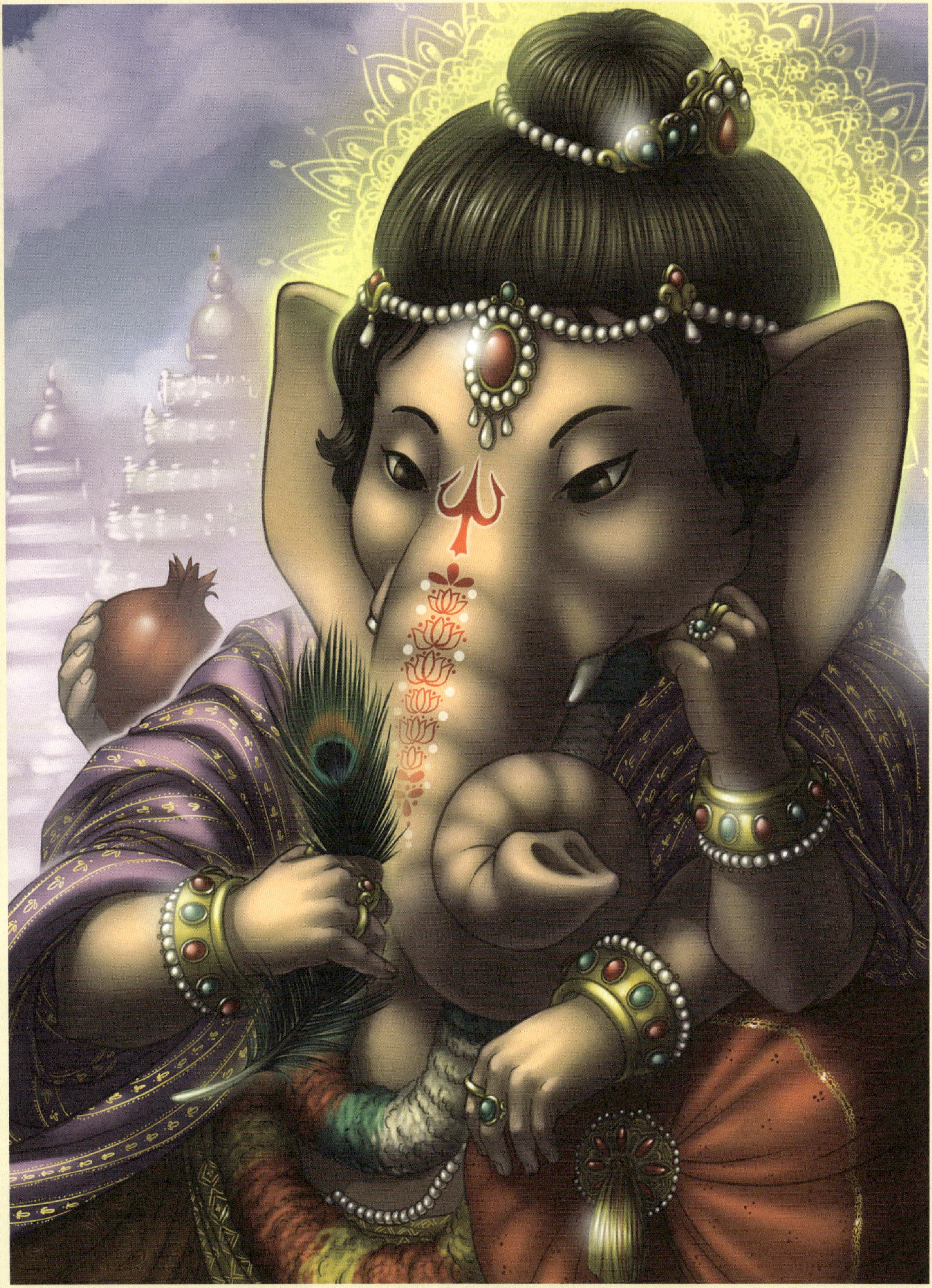

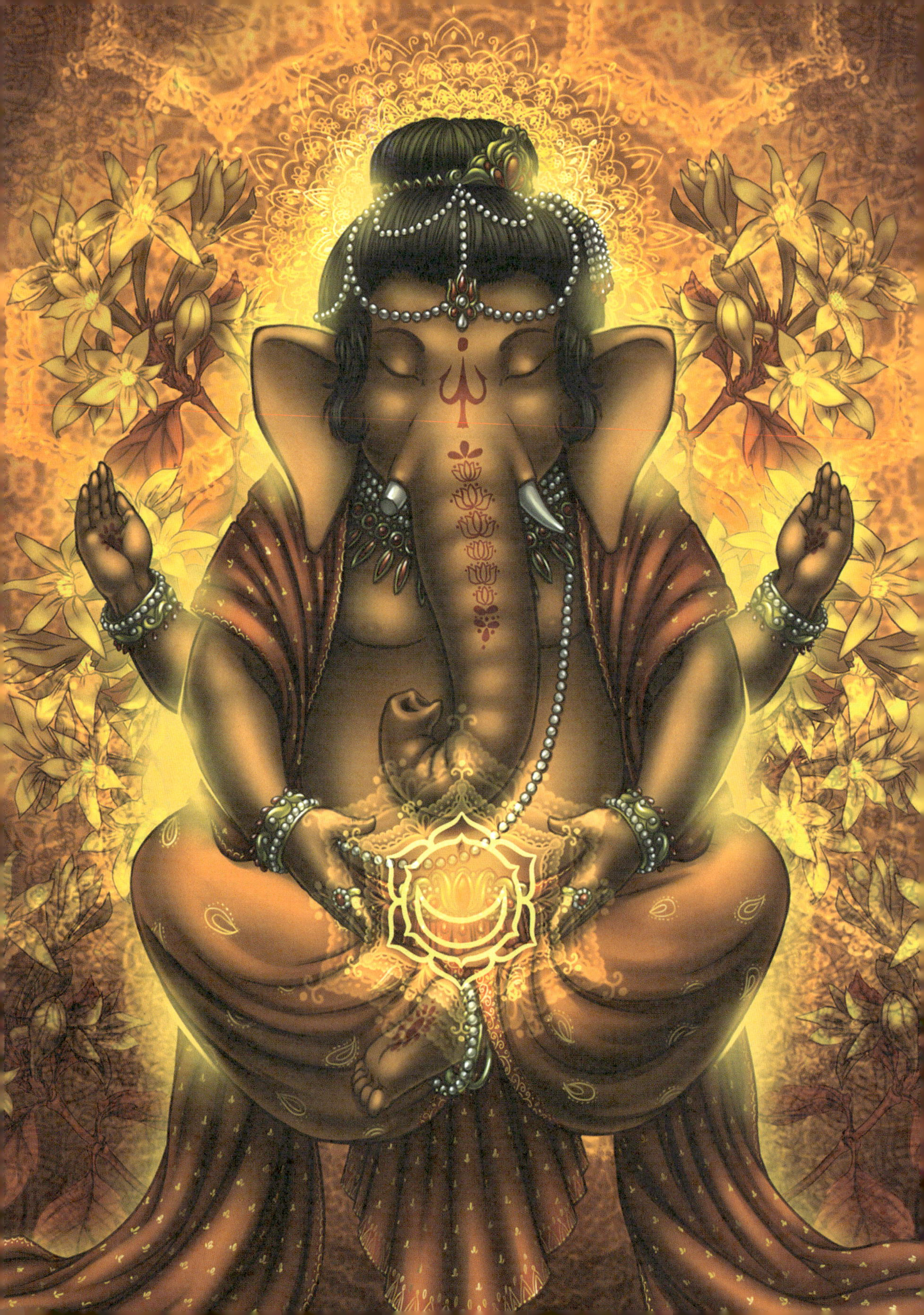

Work with Ganesha for support in stepping up to do the right thing.

Spend more time looking at the good and positive in others rather than what you judge as negative or bad.

Without desire, without fear and without anger are they who take refuge in Me, who are absorbed in Me.
— The Ganesha Gita

Give freely and from your heart.

Ganesha encourages you to maintain a compassionate heart.

Believe in yourself and others to discover the deeper importance of your being.

*Within every soul exists an aspect known as the inner child.
Take a moment to reacquaint yourself with yours.*

*Champion your inner child's emotional life by listening carefully
to what you need and want in your own heart.*

Everything will be okay in the end. If it's not okay, then it's not the end.
— John Lennon

*Karma certainly does not bind him who knows the absence of desire.
Having first understood this, those who want liberation perform action.*
— The Ganesha Gita

Connect deeply to yourself on an emotional level by allowing all of your uncomfortable feelings to reach the surface of your awareness, to be seen and experienced.

Find patience and joy in simple things.

*Focus on your life lessons to reclaim the true meaning of your being.
Free yourself from limiting thoughts and beliefs.*

Ganesha asks that you give yourself permission to be free in order to attain the joy that your heart desires.

Ganesha is clearing the obstacles that have been impeding your progress.

Believe in yourself and your ability to overcome obstacles.

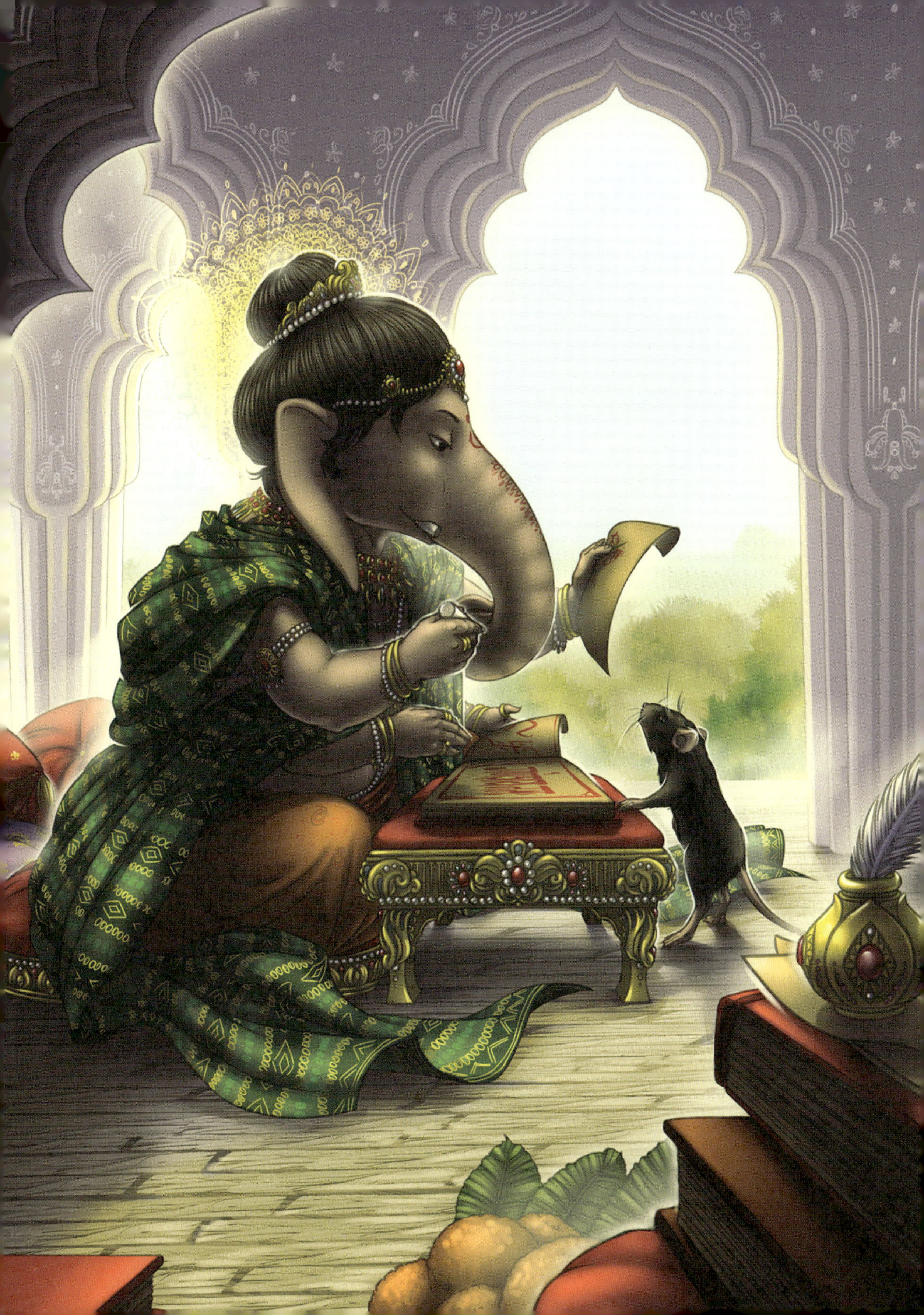

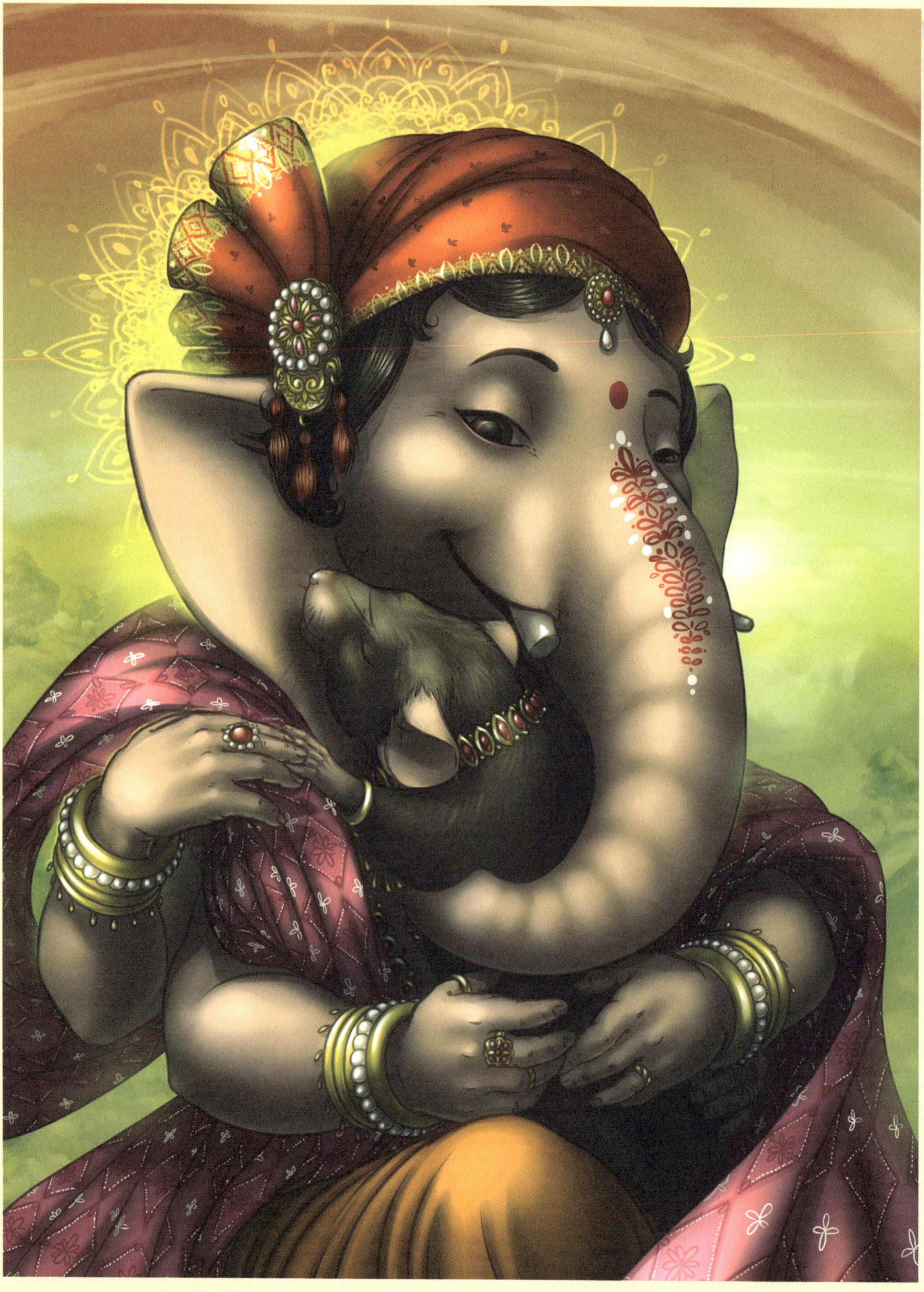

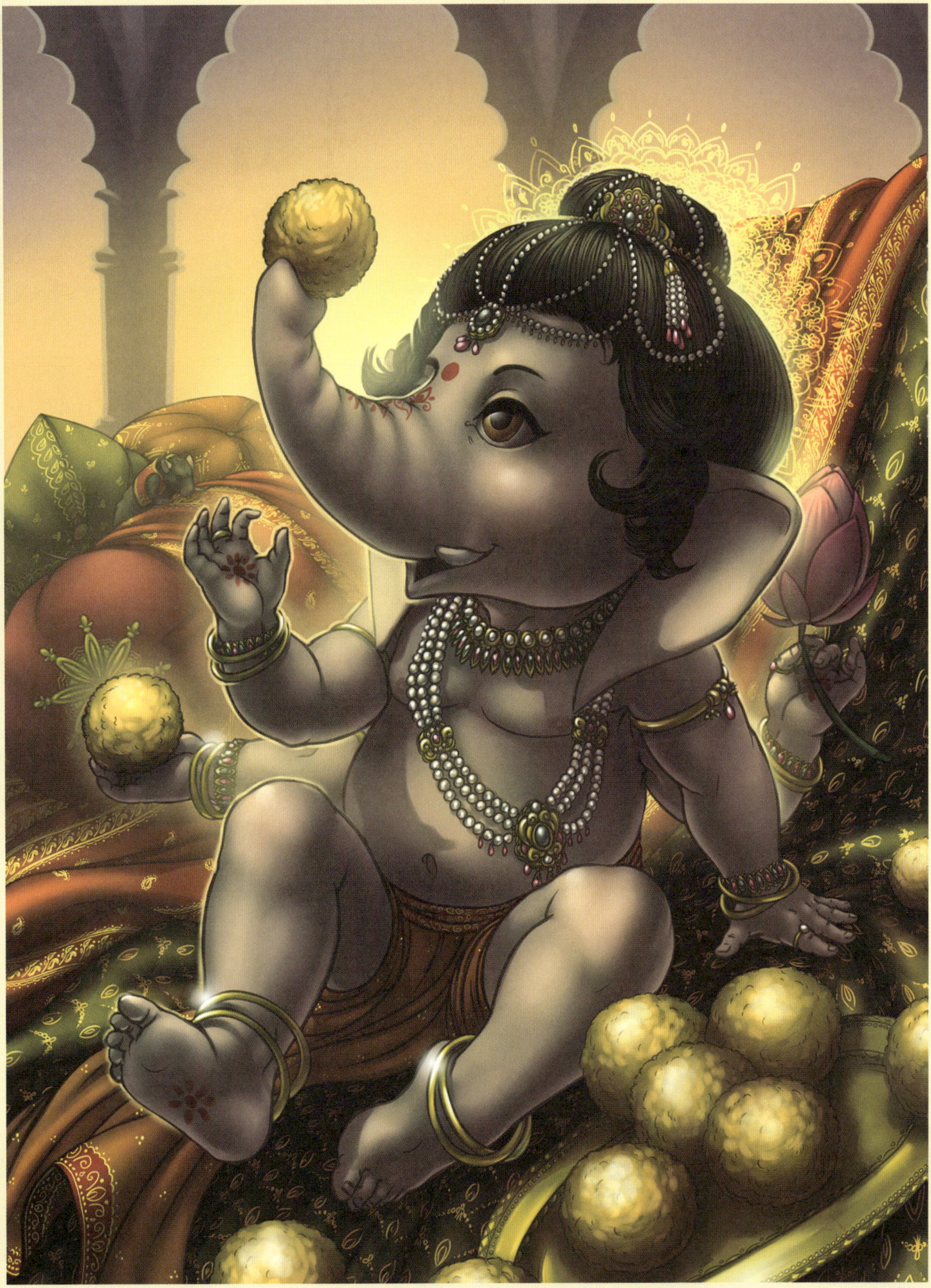

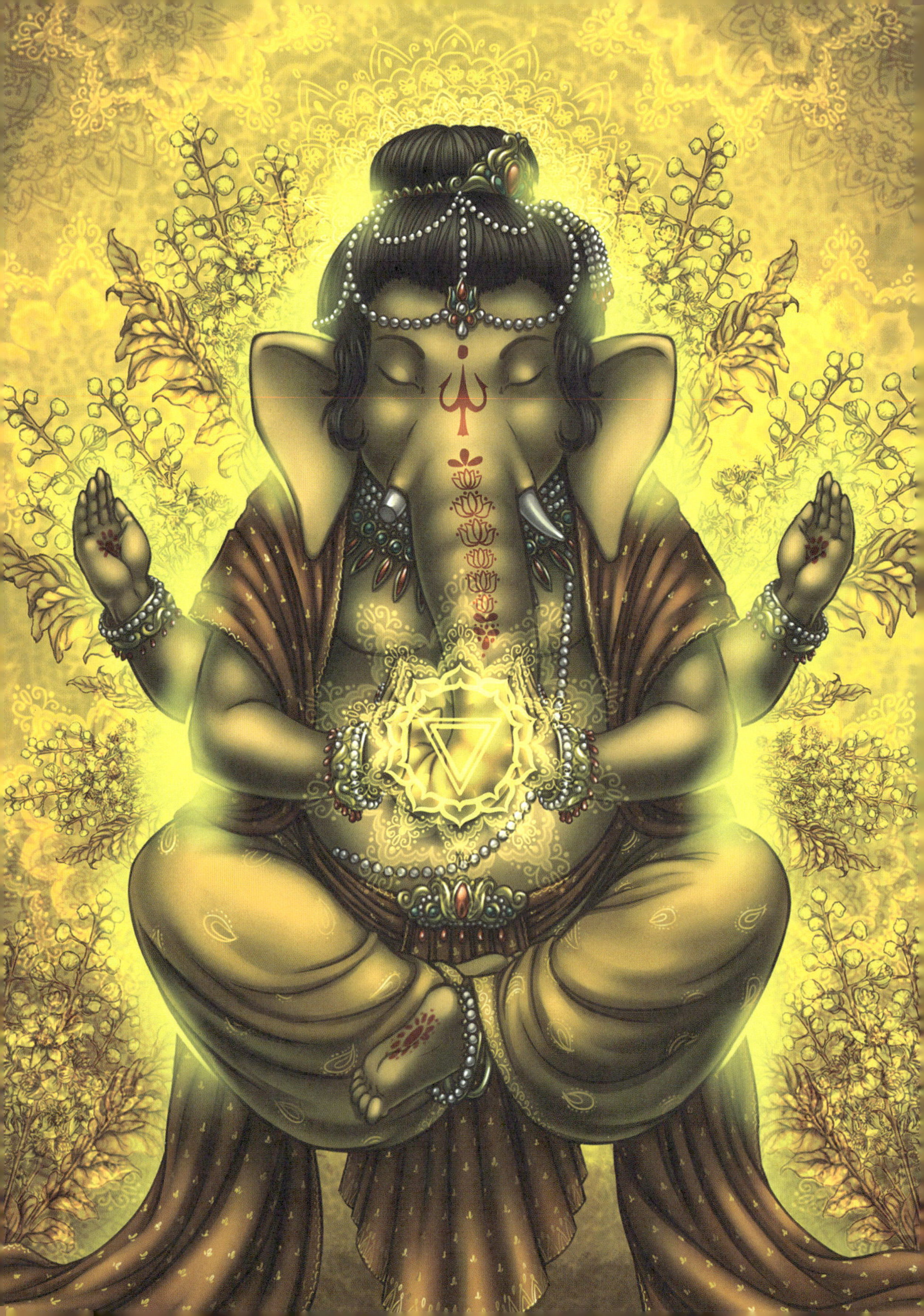

Ask Ganesha to walk beside you and show you what you would benefit from clearing away.

This is a time of soul searching.

A wise man should accomplish difficult or easy tasks with honesty, purpose and intelligence, but without pride and selfishness.
— The Ganesha Purana

*Connecting with those you know love, like and appreciate you restores
the spirit and gives you energy to keep moving forward in this life.*
— Deborah Day

*Work with Ganeshaa and see meditation, consideration
and self-assessment as opportunities to evaluate your direction
and the personal goals that await you.*

Take time to really listen to your heart and inner voice.

Give thanks and gratitude for the things you have accomplished.

Review your goals and regroup accordingly.

Ganesha is asking you to reflect on the benefits of following a specific daily routine for your spirituality.

You can use many tools and techniques throughout your day to preserve or regain tranquility.

In the world of birth and death many difficulties arise, and they are very hard to endure. Remover of obstacles, kindly show me the path to liberation now. How can there be bondage in the realization of You?

— The Ganesha Gita

Ganesha is said to oversee the angels of protection.

Ask Ganesha to surround you with his beautiful energy.

One whose heart is purified by action achieves a unified intellect.
— The Ganesha Gita

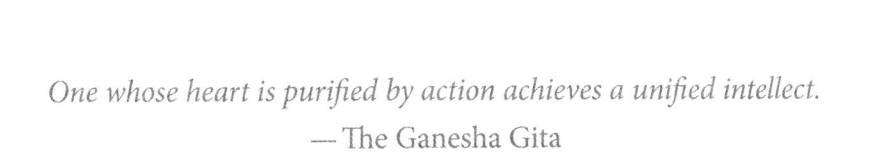

*This is a perfect time to step back from your day-to-day life and
deeply contemplate your motivations, personal principles and values.*

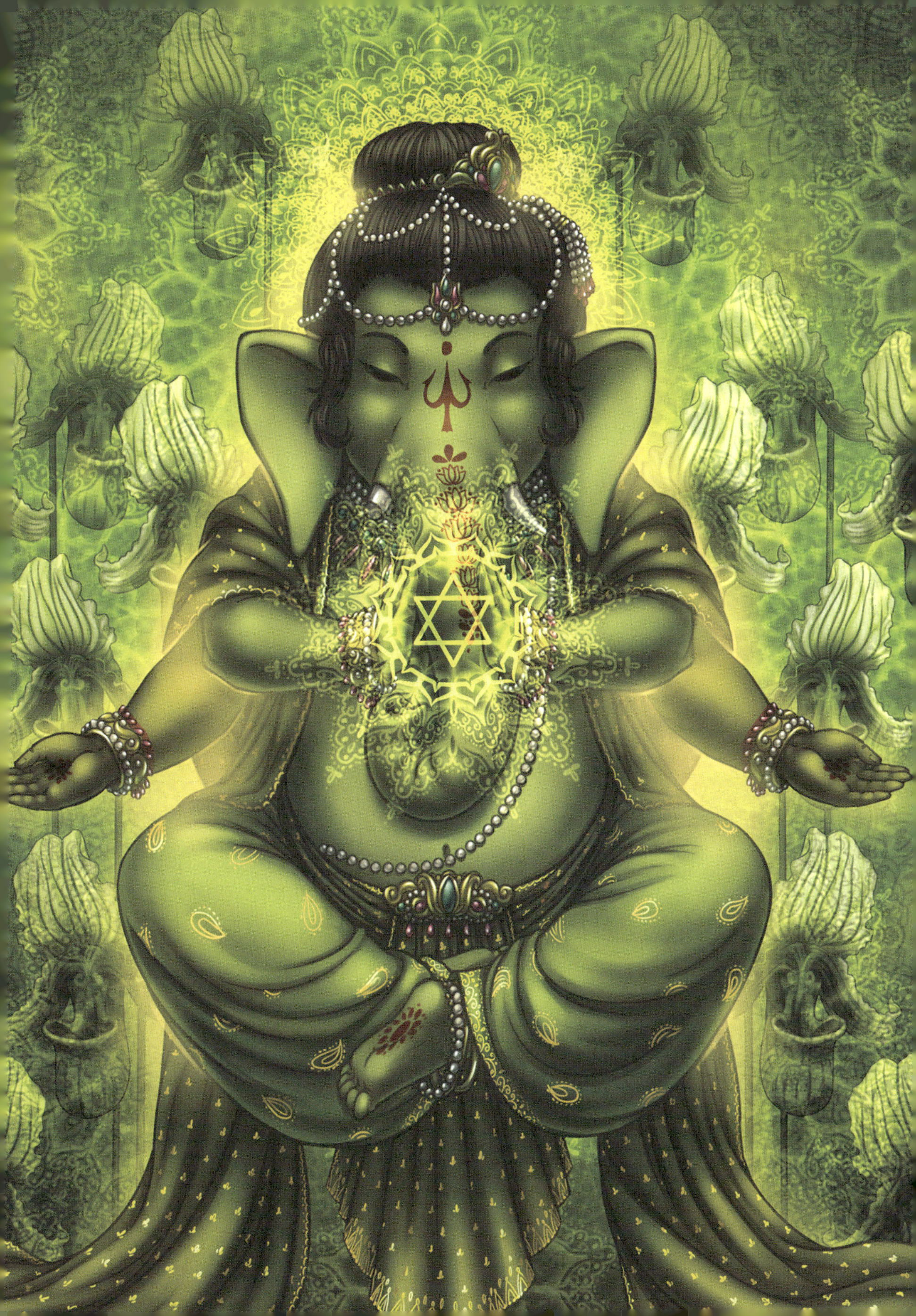

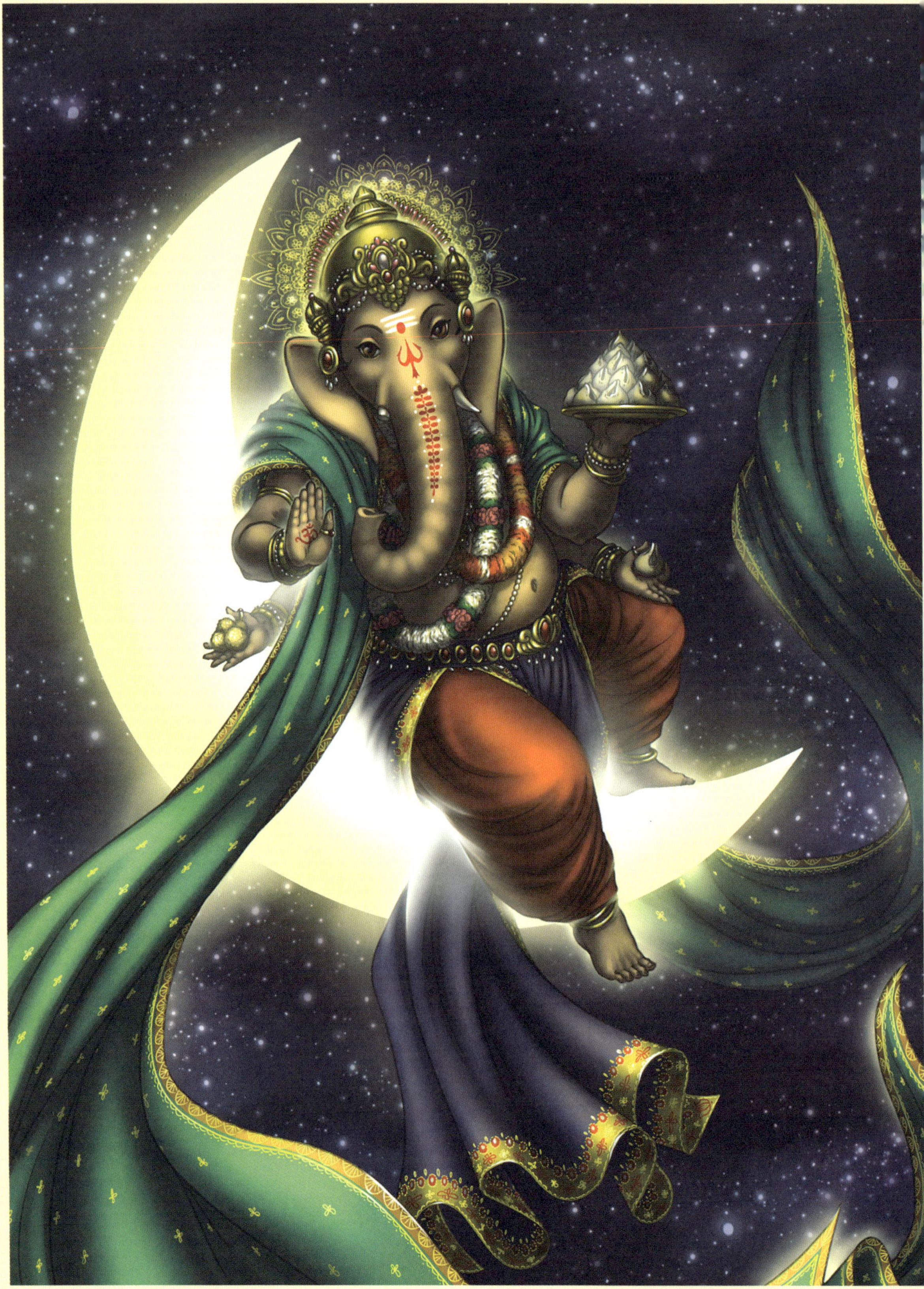

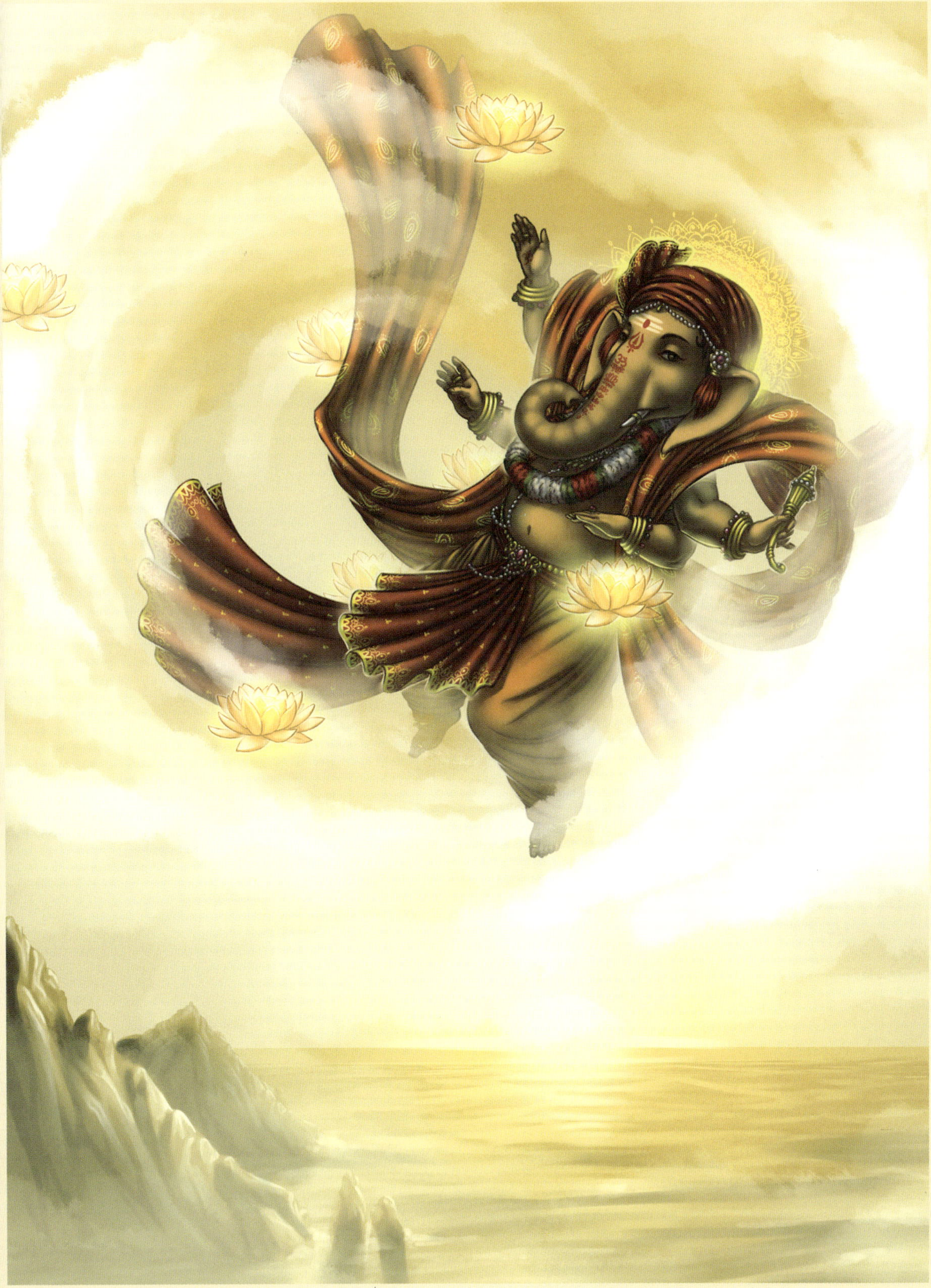

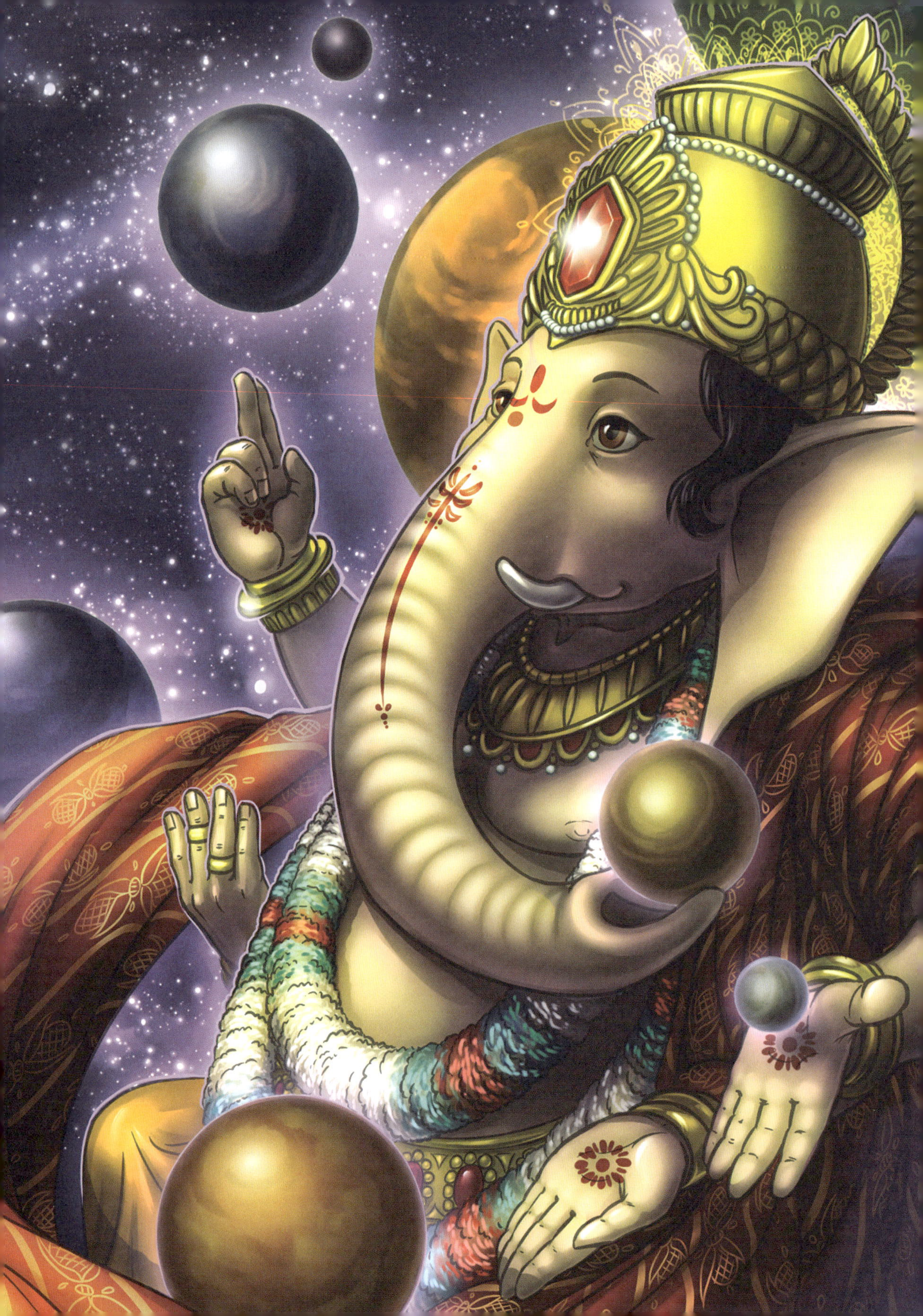

Ganesha's light energy serves to release any negative energy within its field into light.

Do not sit still; start moving now. In the beginning, you may not go in the direction you want, but as long as you are moving, you are creating alternatives and possibilities.
— Rodolfo Costa

A person who has knowledge engages in activity due to the influence of cosmic nature.
— The Ganesha Gita

Ganesha will help you protect your energy and direct it toward the best possible results.

*Ensure your activities are centered on your broader goals and
invest in the right thing at the right time.*

Work with Ganesha to center and release any heaviness you might be feeling.

Ganesha is reminding you to radiate warmth and energy.

Take time to reflect on your personal values and attitudes.

How deserving do you feel?

You are awakening to your personal power and the memory of yourself as a soul.

Every time you criticize yourself, you weaken your resolve.

Loving yourself, accepting yourself and acknowledging your value are the foundations of a balanced solar plexus.

Encourage yourself, believe in yourself, and love yourself. Never doubt who you are.
— Stephanie Lahart

Be willing to powerfully express yourself.

*You have a connection here, not only with this physical body and life,
but with the Divine.*

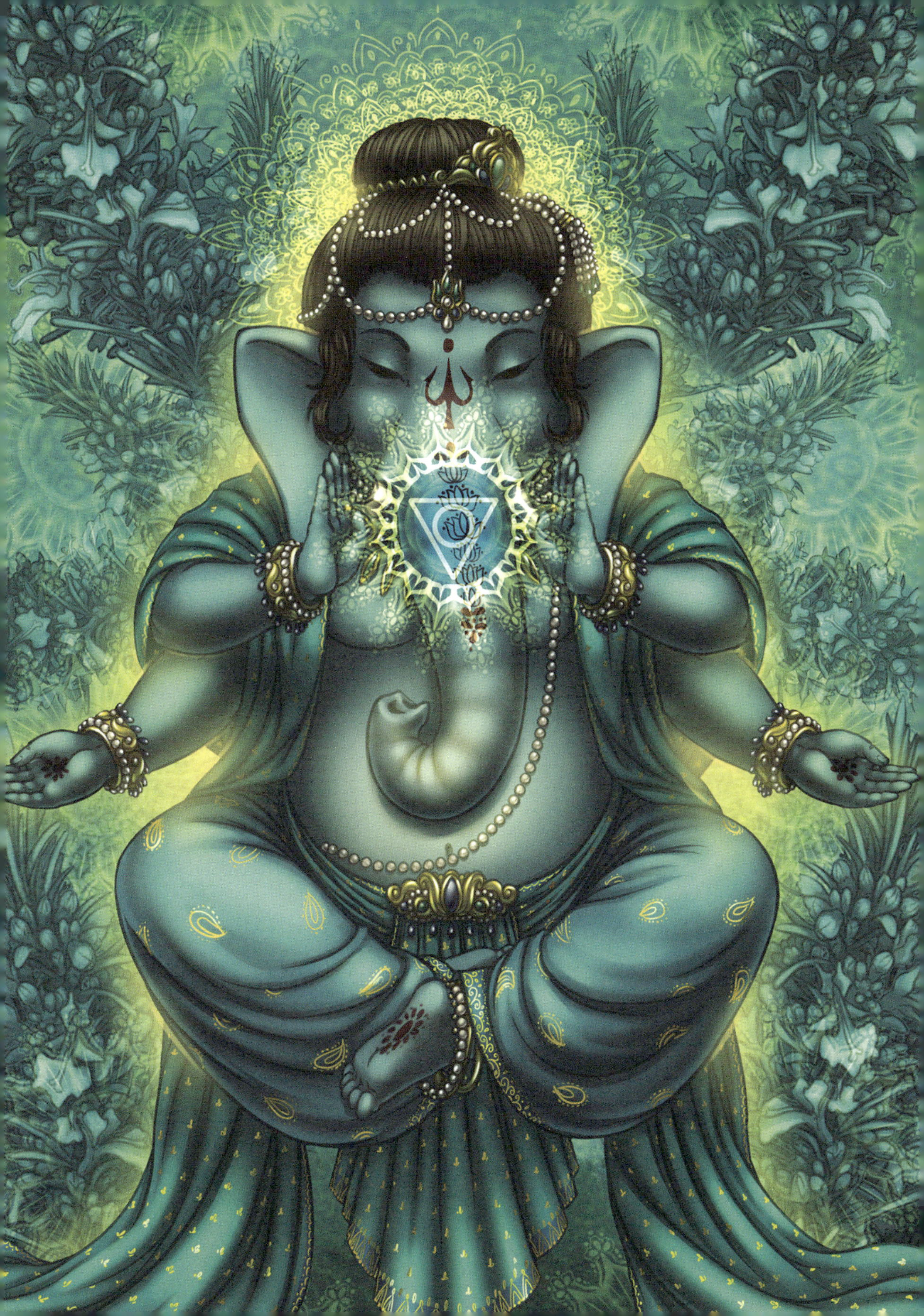

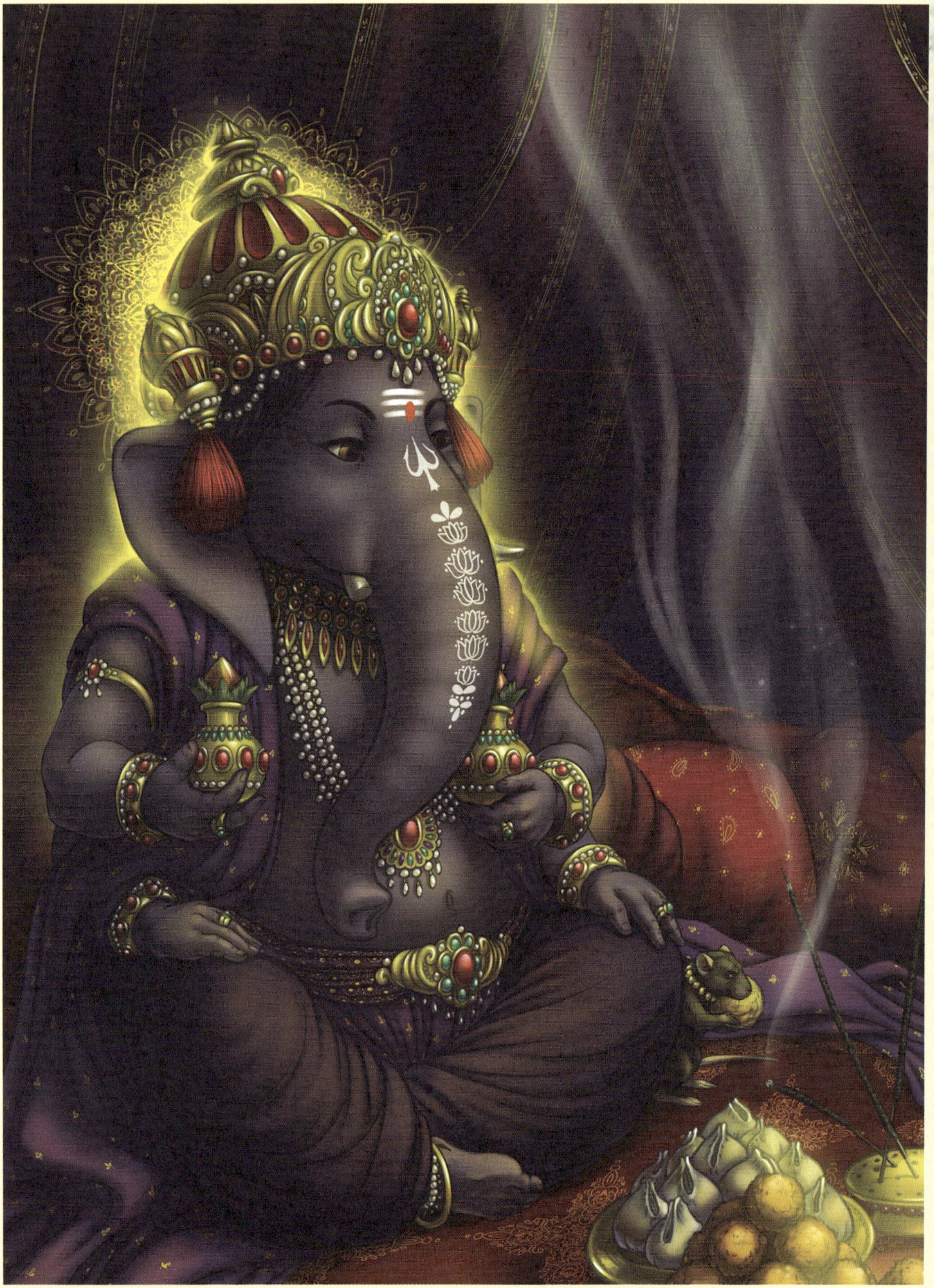

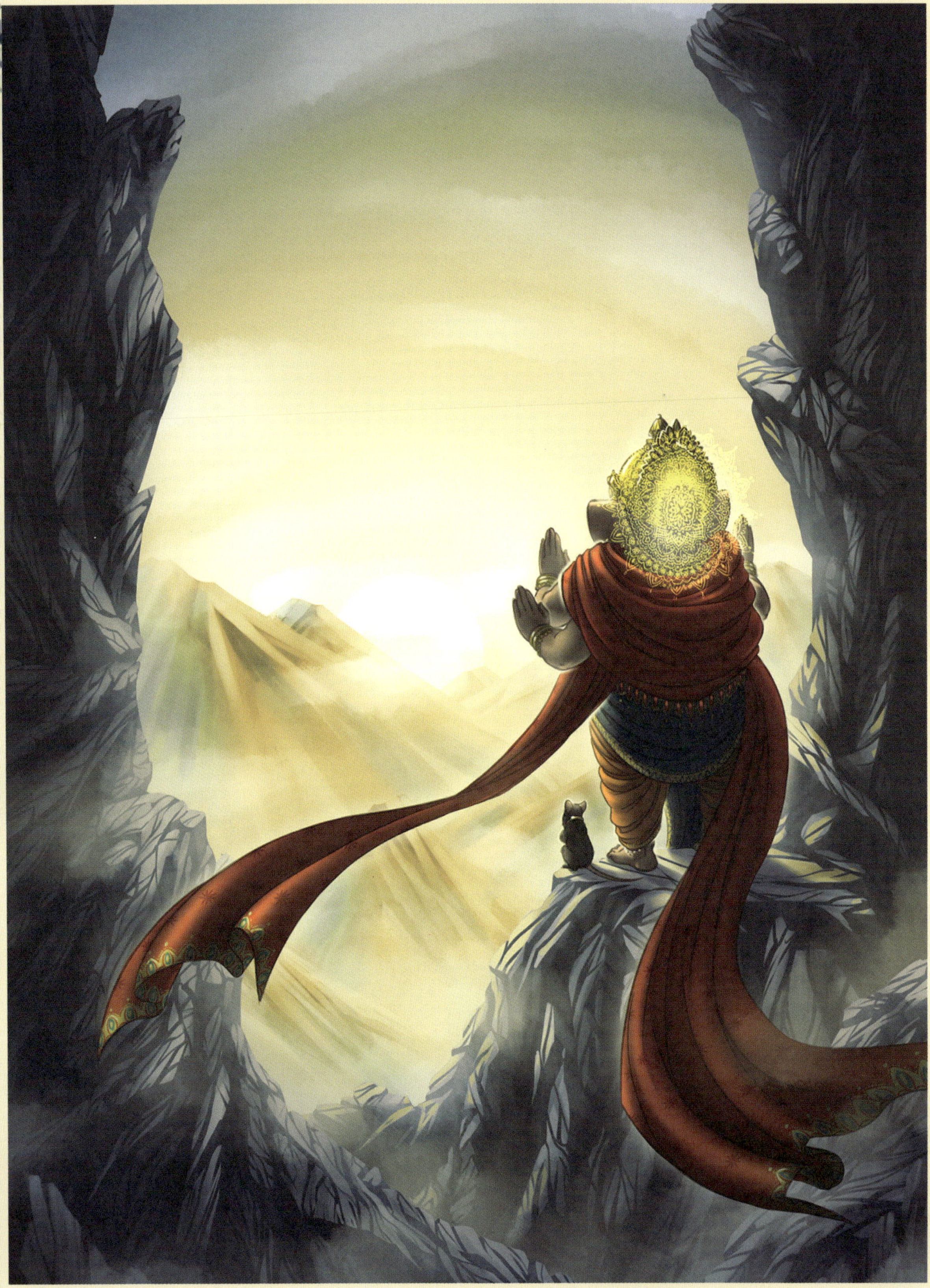

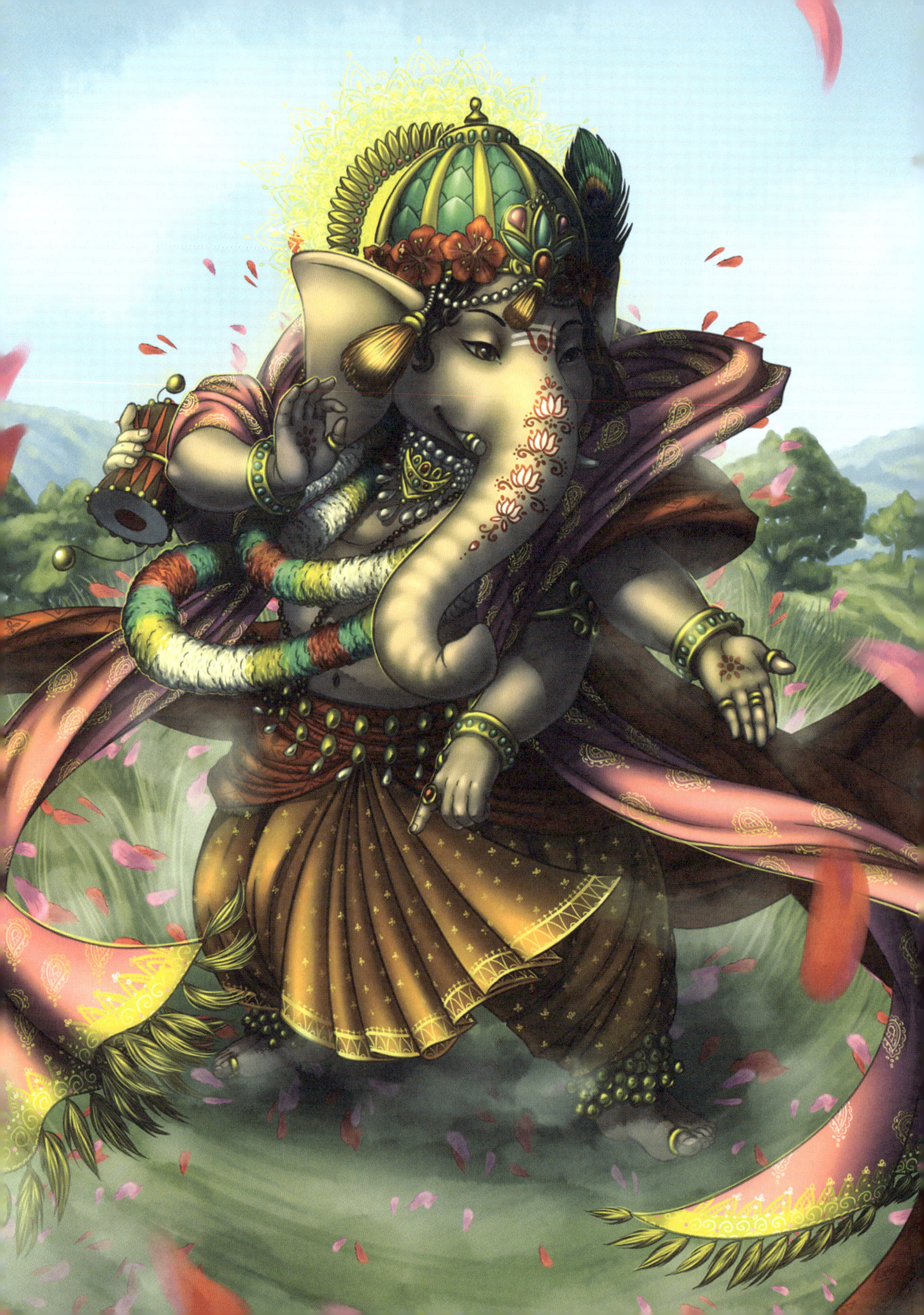

The wise declare the intelligent man as one whose actions are consumed by a vision of the truth. After giving up the desire for results of one's present activities, he will always be satisfied, even without striving.
— The Ganesha Gita

Ganesha is guiding you to the sacred truth that you are a divine being, here to give and receive love.

*When the heart chakra is open, you are able to create a safe and
supportive, loving environment.*

Have faith that open and honest communication can bring resolution.

Convey your thoughts in an understandable, brief and well-thought-out manner.

Guidance from the Divine can always be trusted.

*You are intelligent with a good imagination
and accurate perceptions.*

> *Through attachment to the good soul there arises good qualities and the disappearance of misfortunes. This sort of good fortune is gained in this world and in the next. Material fortune is easy to obtain, but association with the good soul is hard to find.*
> — The Ganesha Gita

Ganesha shares his purple hue to assist you with the spiritual journey inside yourself.

Cultivate an optimistic mind, use your imagination, always consider alternatives, and dare to believe that you can make possible what others think is impossible.
— Rodolfo Costa

Listen! For those who know their own self Brahman emanates everywhere.
— The Ganesha Gita

Set a clear goal for how you would like to connect with your higher self.

Choose to live fully and achieve real enlightenment — where all things are possible.

A person who has the same attitude in happiness, pain, exaltation, hatred, satiation and in thirst knows Me as omnipresent and knows all beings through the identity of the self.
— The Ganesha Gita

Ganesha enjoins you not to lose faith while you wait for things to come to fruition.

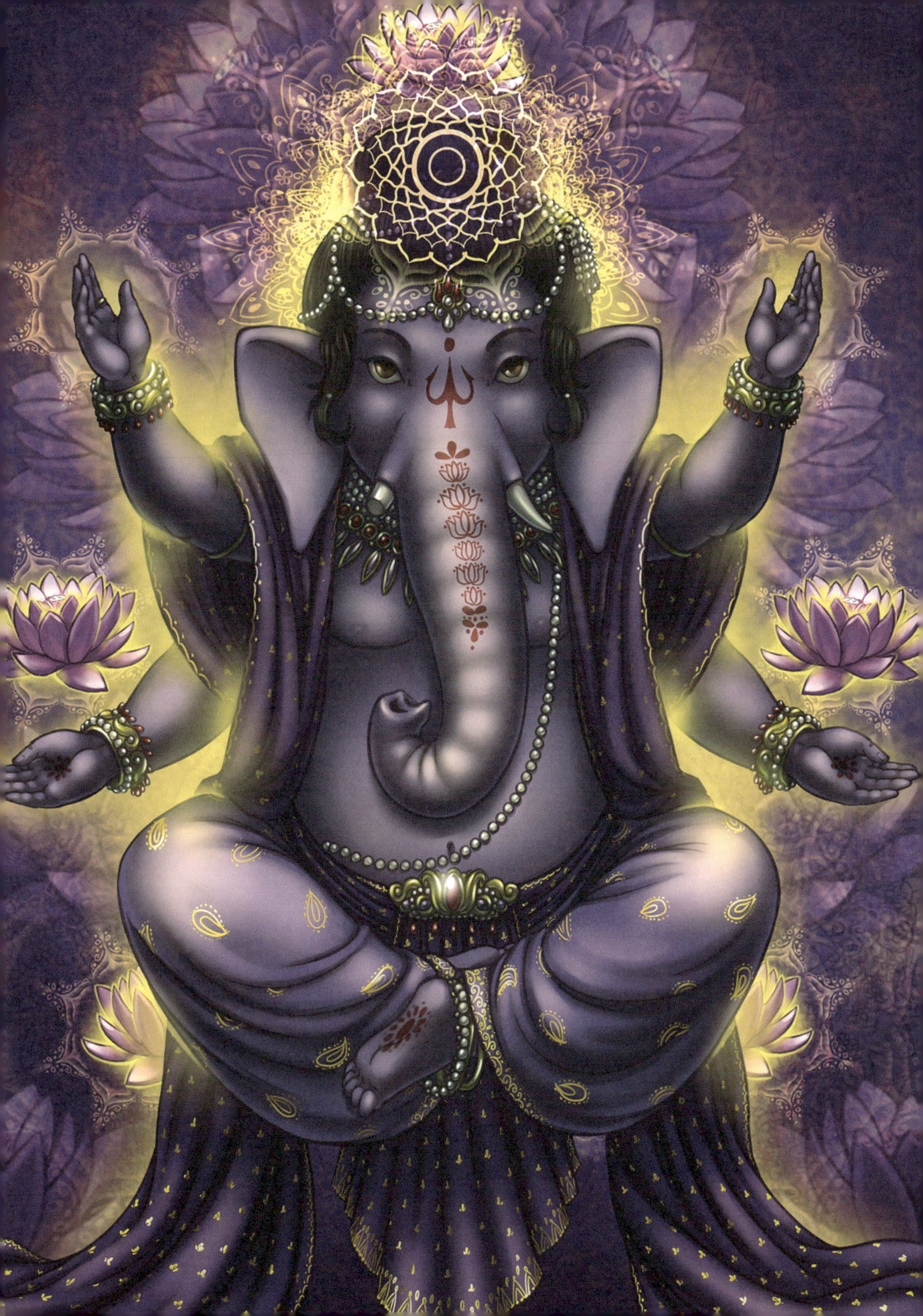

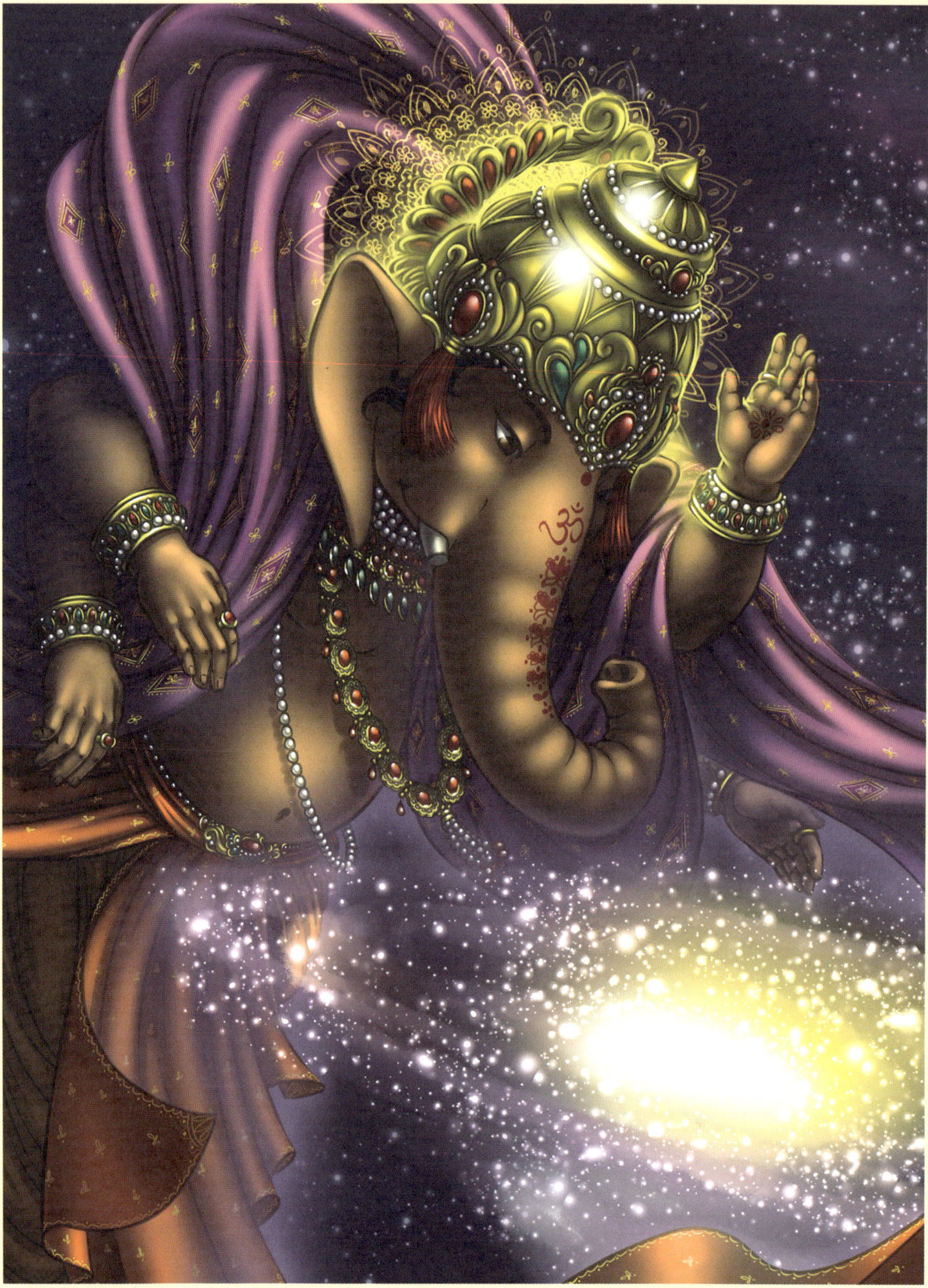

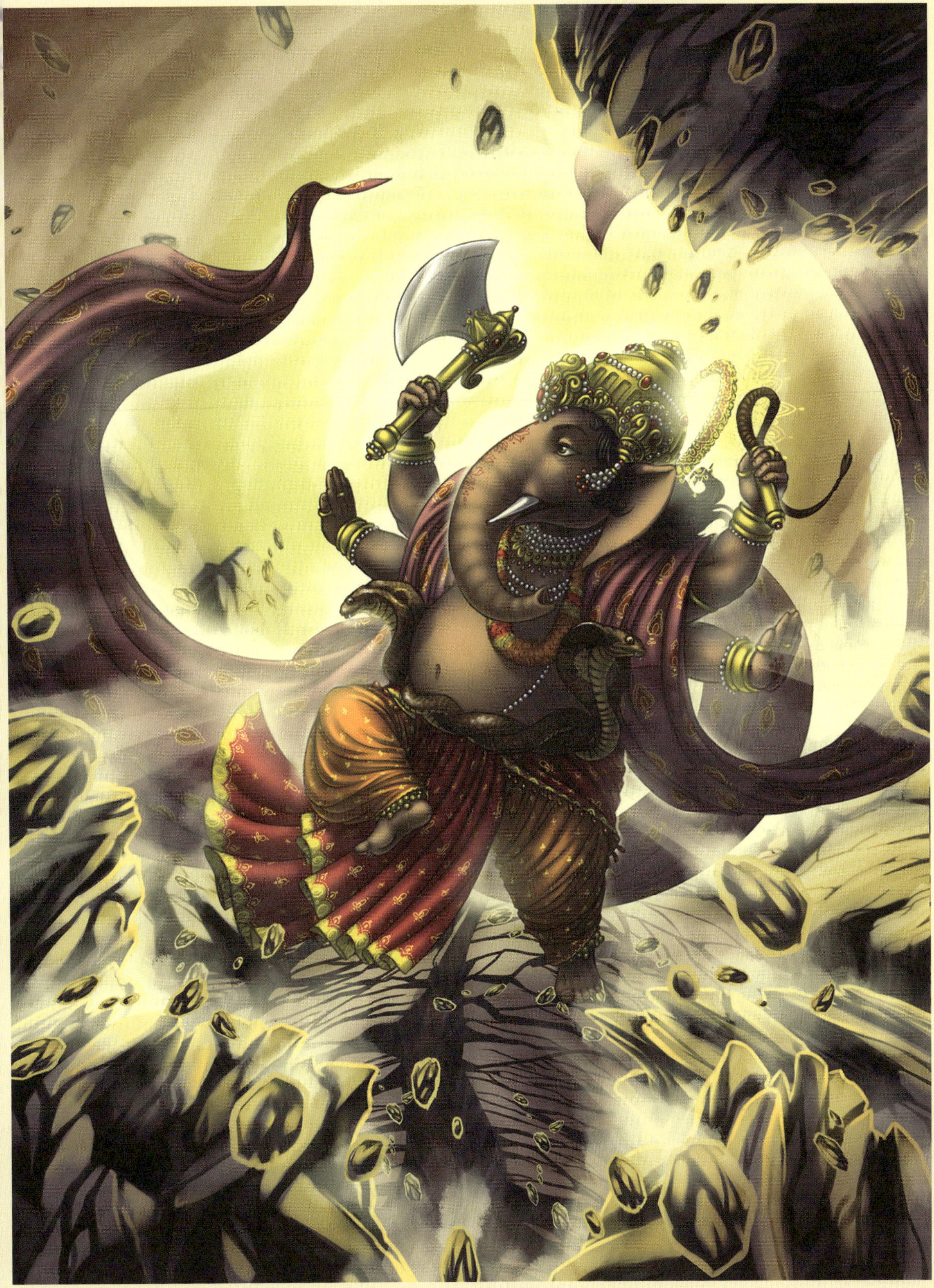

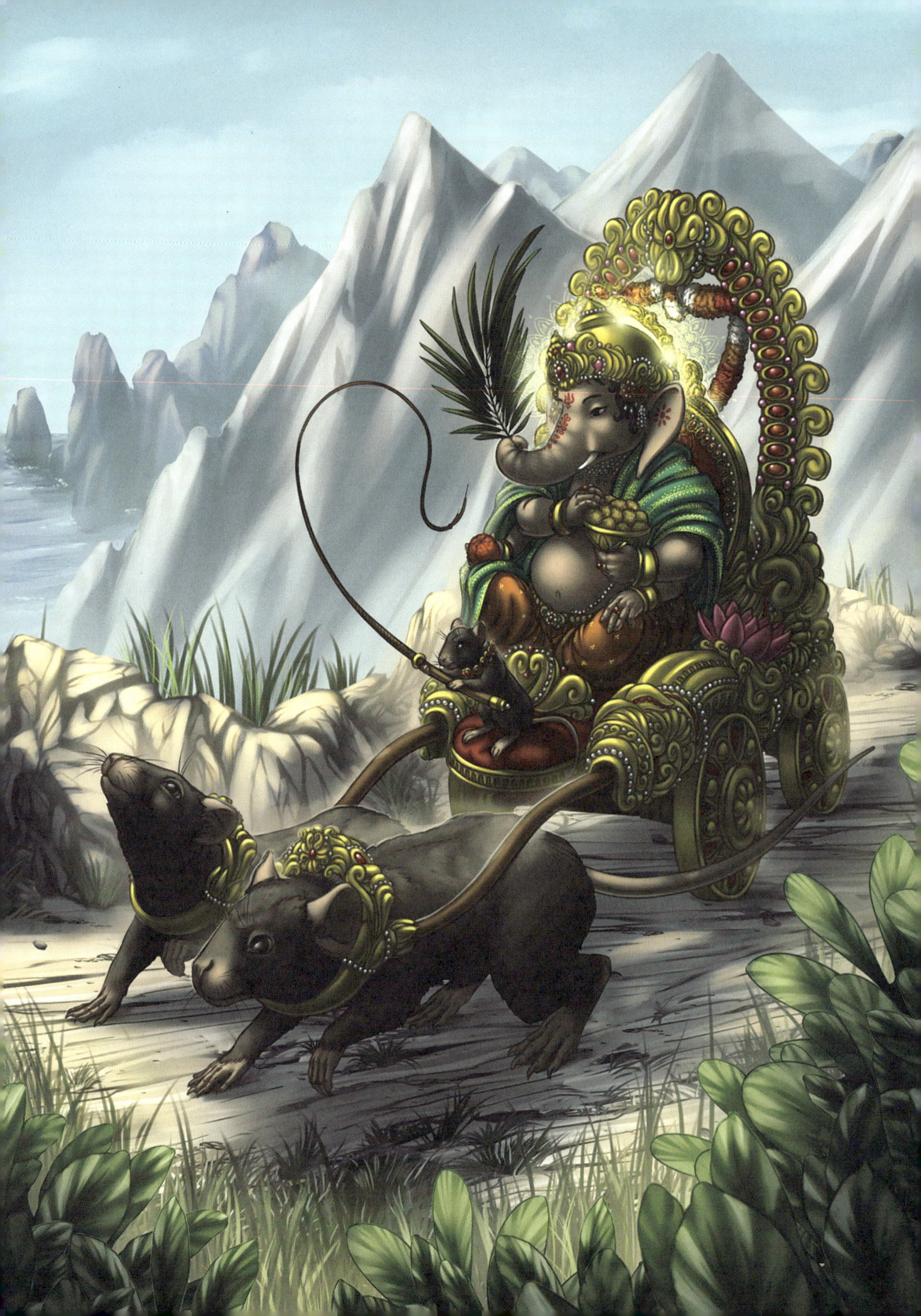

Be grateful, focus on the present and do what you can with what you have.

It is important to remember that circumstances are neither good nor bad but always neutral.

Your thoughts determines how your day will go.

Take positive action to shift back to happiness.

Every day is a gift.

What makes you happiest?

Aum! Let us listen with our ears to that which is auspicious, adorable one. Let us perceive with our eyes what is holy and auspicious. With strong, stable body and limbs, may we seek the divine grace and accept the noble order of all our life.
— Ganapati Atharvashirsha

At the root of all misery is unfulfilled desire.
— Scott Hahn

Time is not something that can be saved for later.

What exactly do you want in this situation?

Motivate yourself by taking time out to rejuvenate.

Ask Ganesha for the strength to work through what is happening.

The soul can send you messages through symbols, synchronicity, hunches, sudden inspiration, dreams, and direct channeling.

Watch for synchronicities and opportunities. Trust your instincts and pay attention as messages can arise from a variety of sources.

Protect me. Protect the speakers. Protect the hearers. Protect the givers. Protect the holders. Protect the disciple that repeats. Protect that in the east. Protect that in the south. Protect that in the west. Protect that in the north. Protect that above. Protect that below. Everywhere protect! Protect me everywhere!

— Ganapati Upanisad

When your heart is open, you will find your actions match your words.

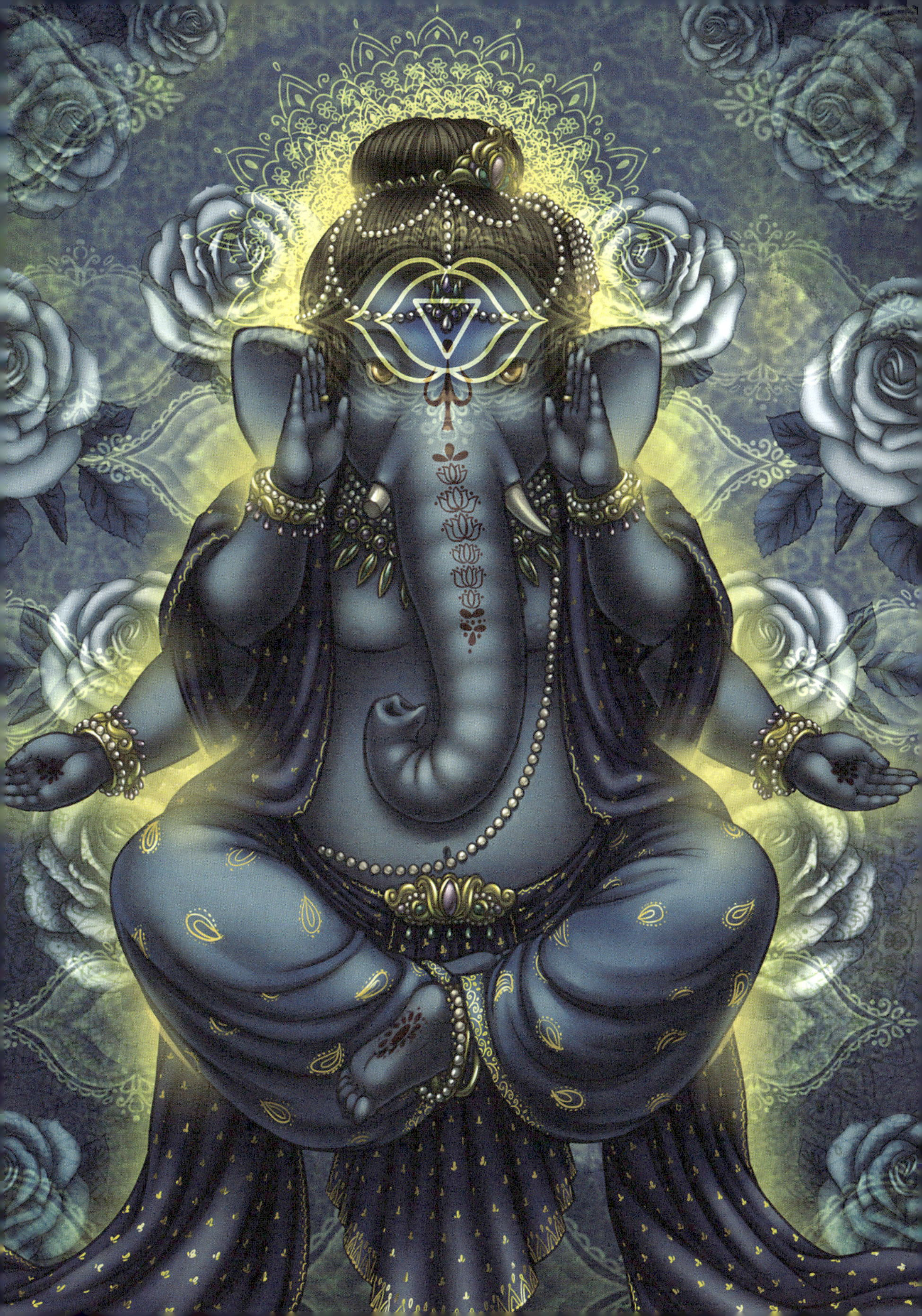

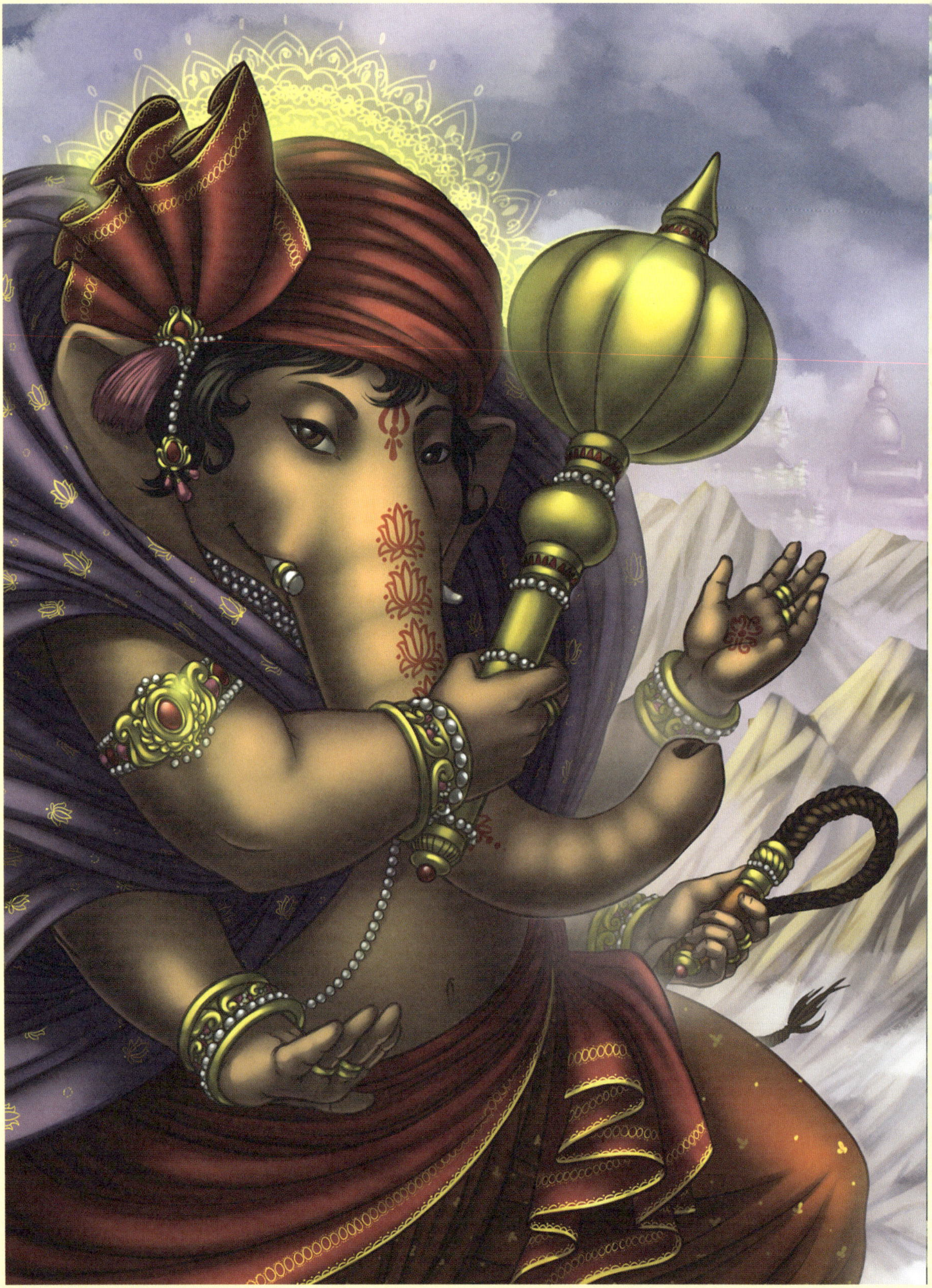

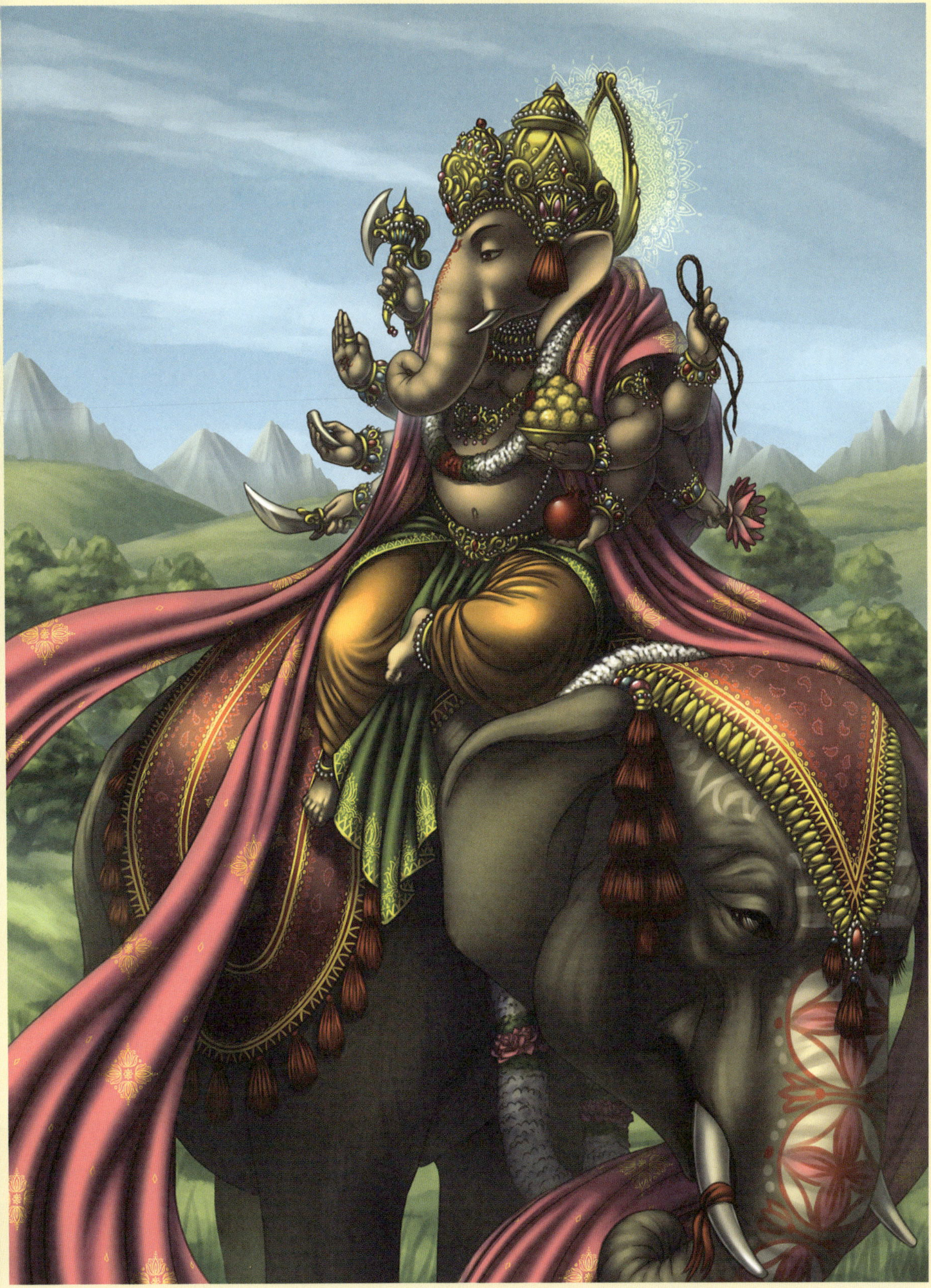

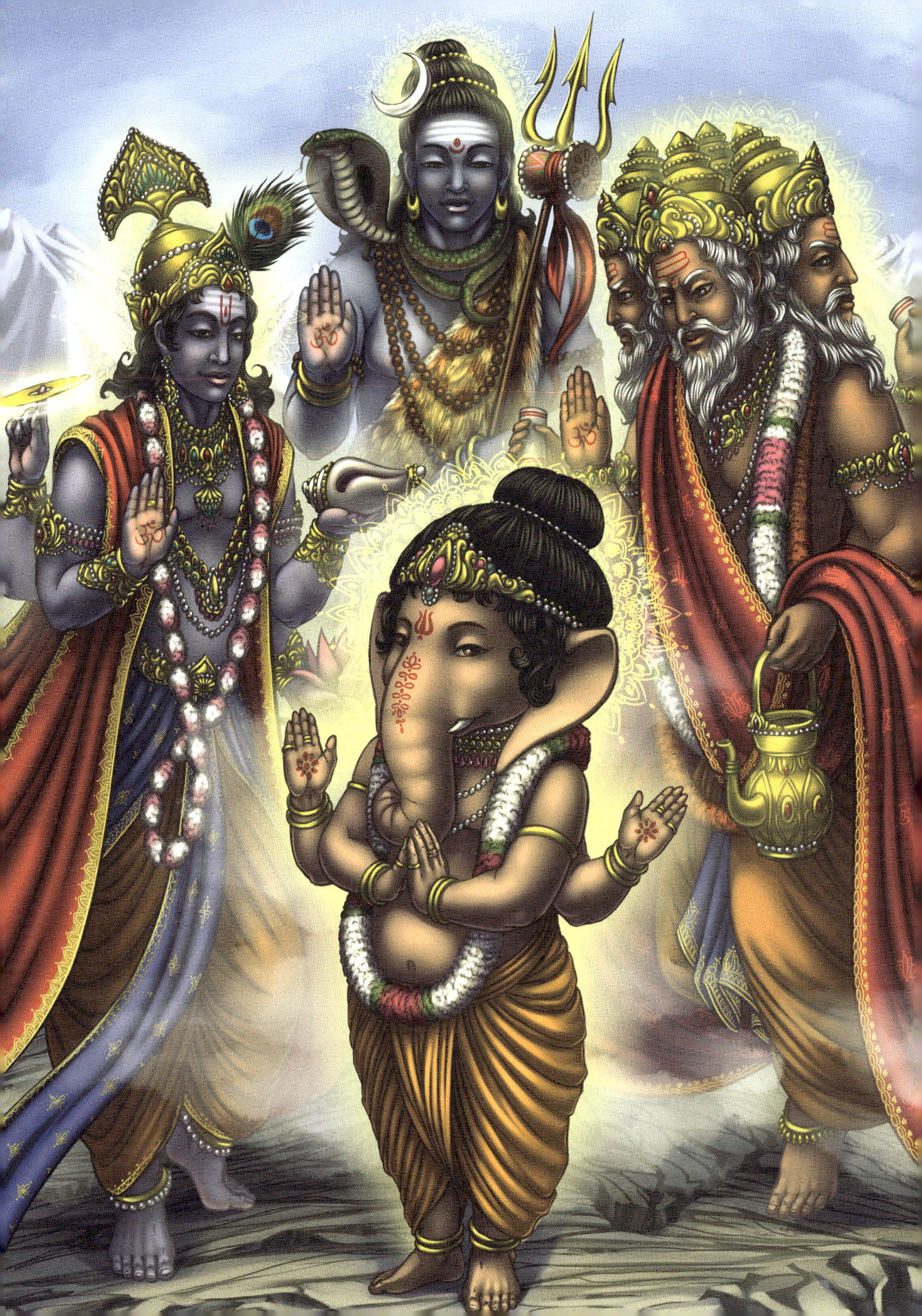

*Rely on your own vast array of abilities to tackle your problems.
Know that Ganesha is supporting you in this process.*

Listen to the small still voice within.

If you want to reach your true potential, it's much more effective to ignite a new passion for life than to dwell on past problems.
— Neil A. Fiore

Eliminate everything in your life that is not essential to your transformation.

Remember that you are created from the perfection of divine light and love.

*Ganesha prompts you to believe that you truly can handle this
with integrity and grace.*

*Music has the power to unite communities and cultures.
Listening to music can heal, hearten and support your soul.*

*Let us think of the one-toothed, let us meditate on the crooked trunk,
may that tusk direct us.*
— Ganapati Upanisad

Tune in to uplifting or calming music to create space for greater contemplation. In turn, you will gain more clarity about what you are creating in your life.

Ganesha invites you to incorporate music into your life in a way that will augment your spiritual expansion.

O Lord Ganesha, of curved trunk, large body, and with the brilliance of a million suns, please make all my works free of obstacles, always.
　— Vakratunda Mahakaya Mantra

Empower yourself by nurturing yourself and then, from a healthy place, help others.

Deal with issues as they arise. Brainstorm practical, easy solutions that will fix a problem with minimal drama.

Keep track of your paces, for your walk makes marks. Each mark is a reward or a stumbling block. Learn to look at the step you have made and the step you have not made yet. This brings you close to Me.
— A letter from Ganesha, by Satgura Sivaya Subramuniyaswami

*Ganesha asks you to forgive those from the past who have hurt you,
and to be willing to forgive yourself, too.*

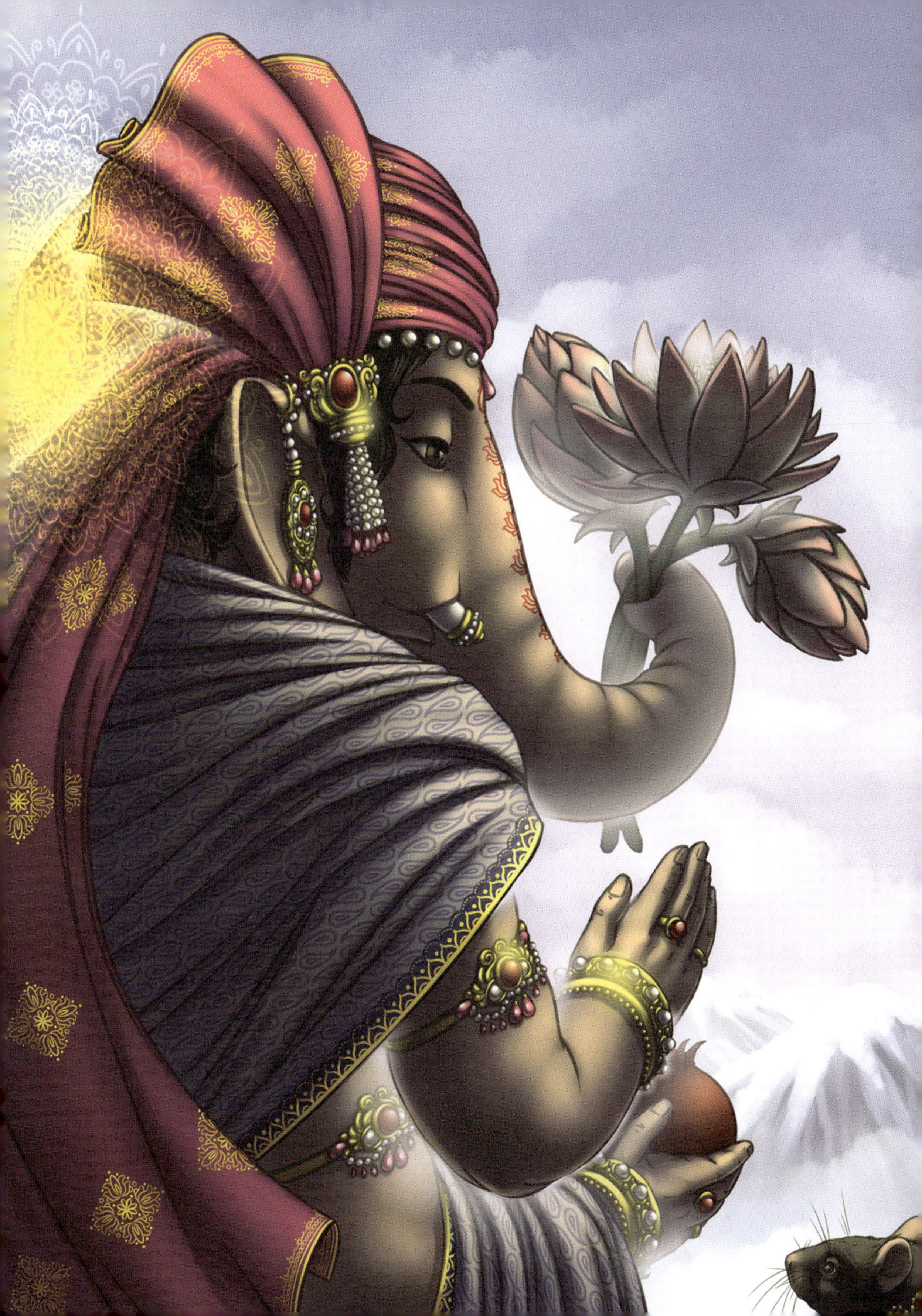

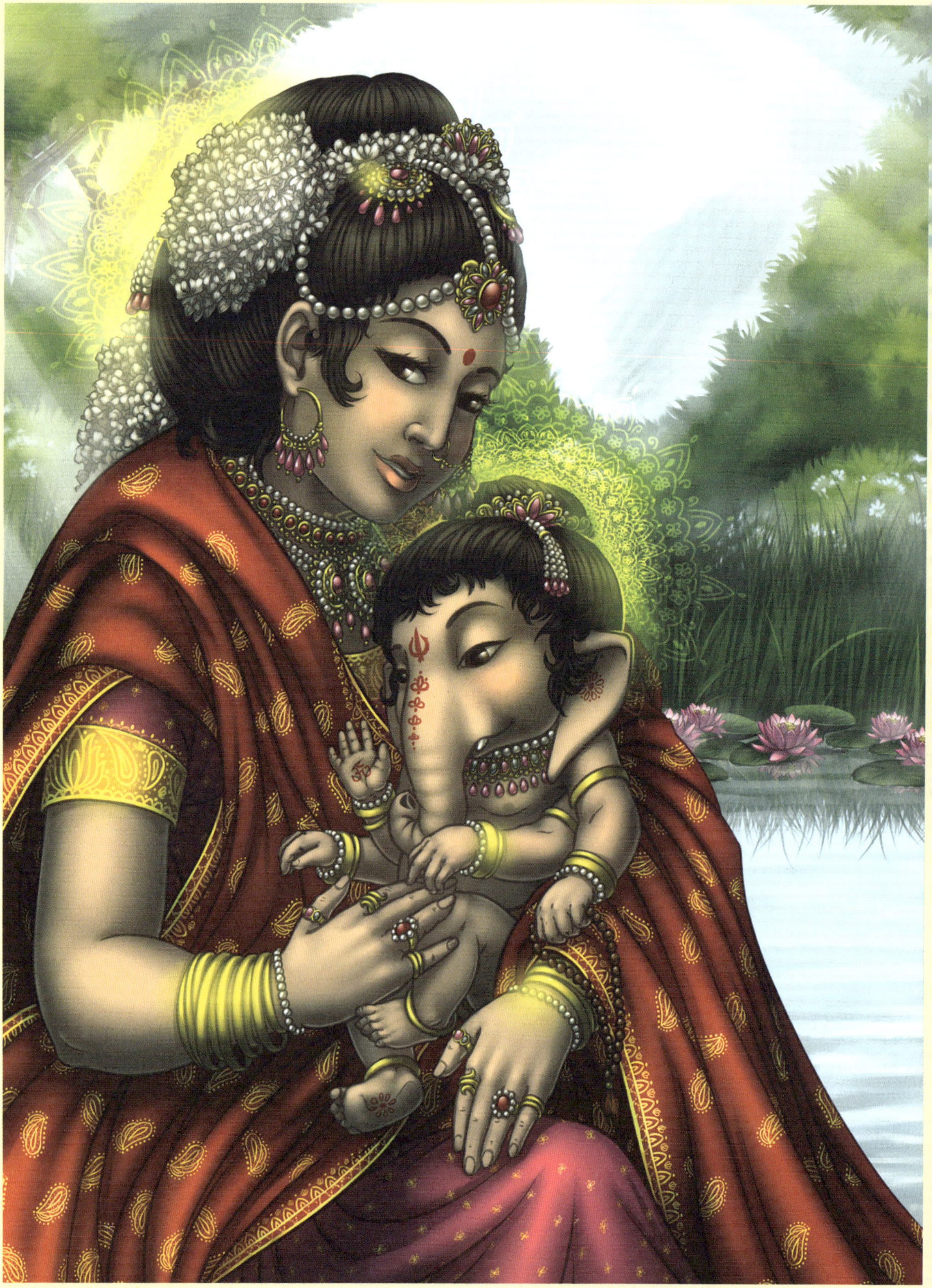

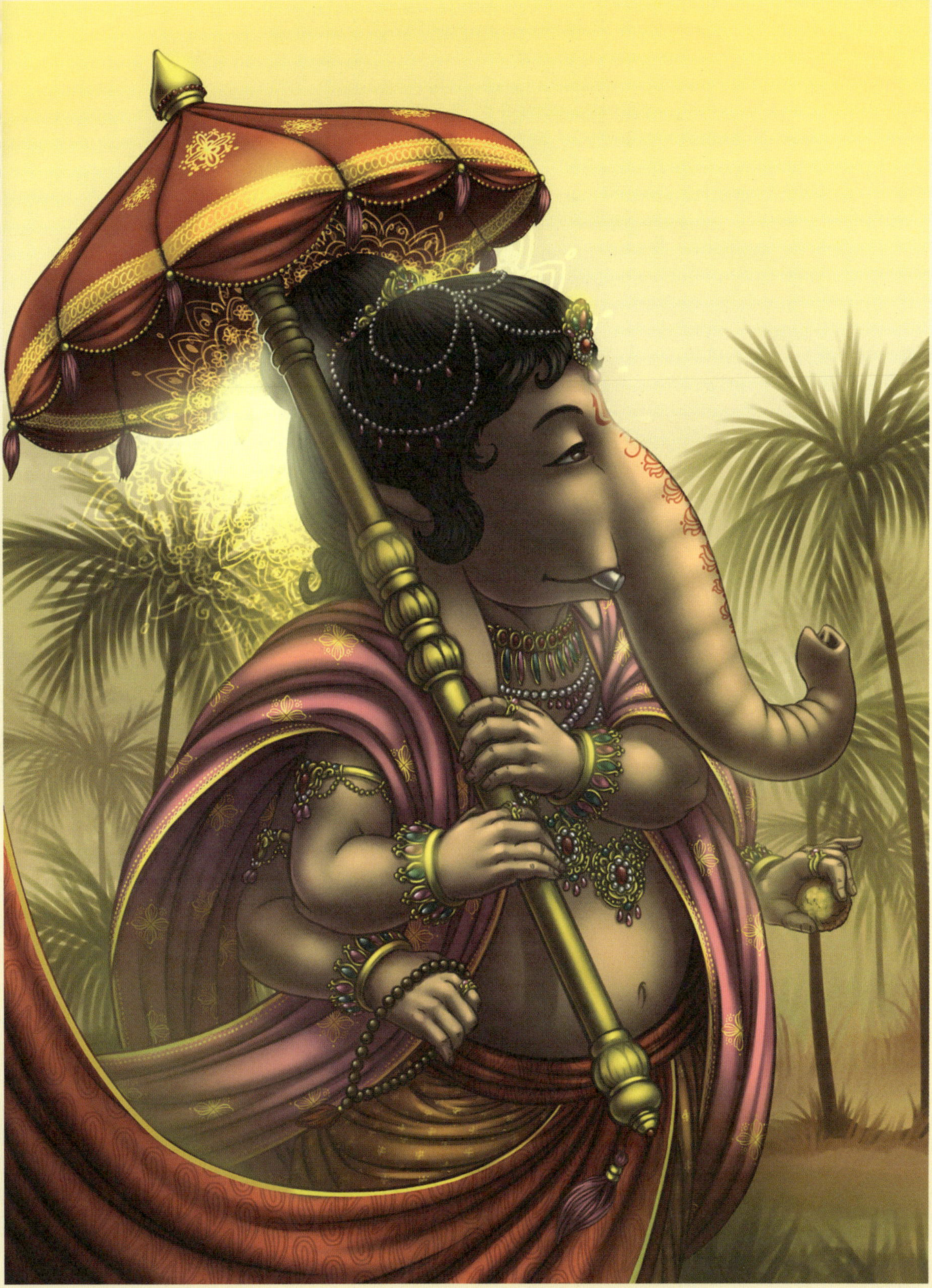

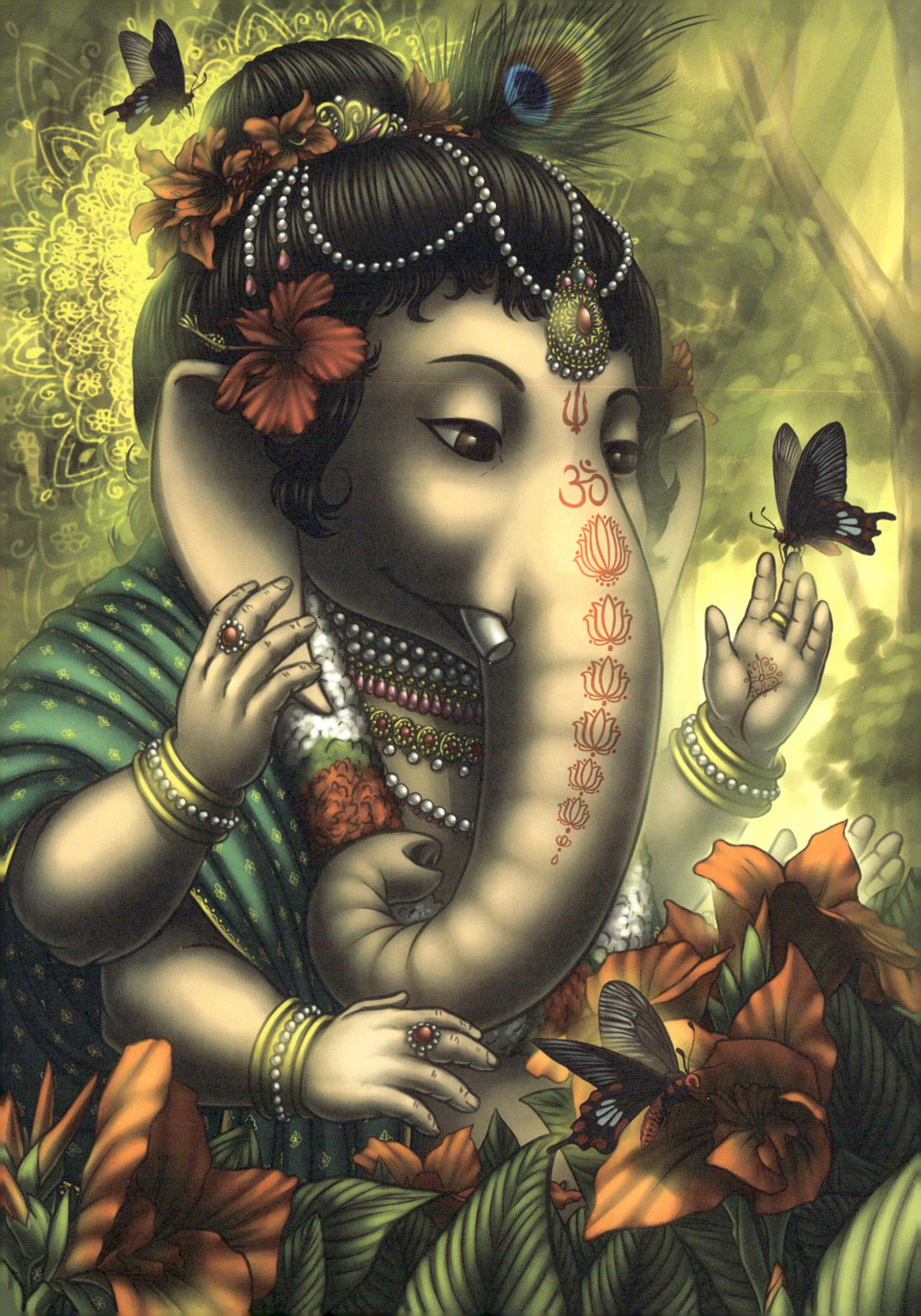

The noble-minded encourage what is beautiful in people and discourage what is ugly in them. Little people do just the opposite.

— Confucius

Your contentment in life improves dramatically when you harness your ability to look at the world from a more spiritual perspective.

Love without judgment and live without predetermined opinions.

Your soul is leading you to myriad discoveries about who you truly are and what you came here to achieve in this lifetime.

Ganesha urges you to focus less on having, and more on being.

Belonging seeks to solve the predicament of the ego's perceived separation.

*There are many positive aspects to belonging: you develop your
ability to love, connect, bond, share, and care for others.*

Ganesha is here to help you be a positive part of a community.

Learn to trust, ask for help and rely on others.

Actively develop your spirituality and consciously work with the Divine, and you will experience positive flow-on effects in all areas of your existence.

You're going to make it; You're going to be at peace; You're going to create, and love, and laugh, and live; You're going to do great things.
— Germany Kent

*When you stay connected to your spiritual nature,
you have a more serene mind.*

Now, the door of a house is a very important place. It separates your house from hostile outer environs. Ganesha stands there to protect you and your dwelling against all possible evil forces. He is a great God at the gate.

— B.R. Kishore

Be willing to let go of preconceived ideas. Allow your heart to be centered and in a place of peace.

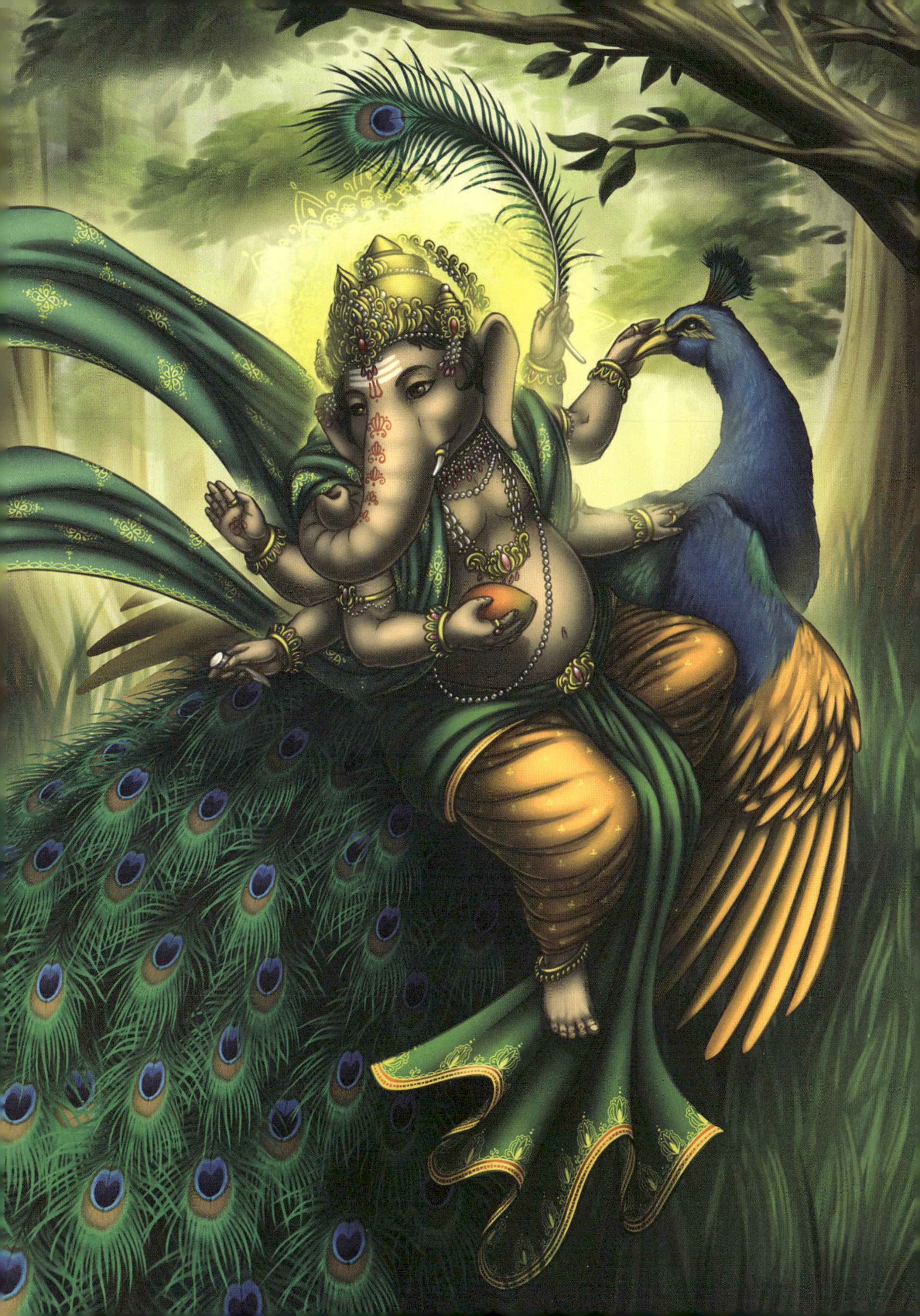

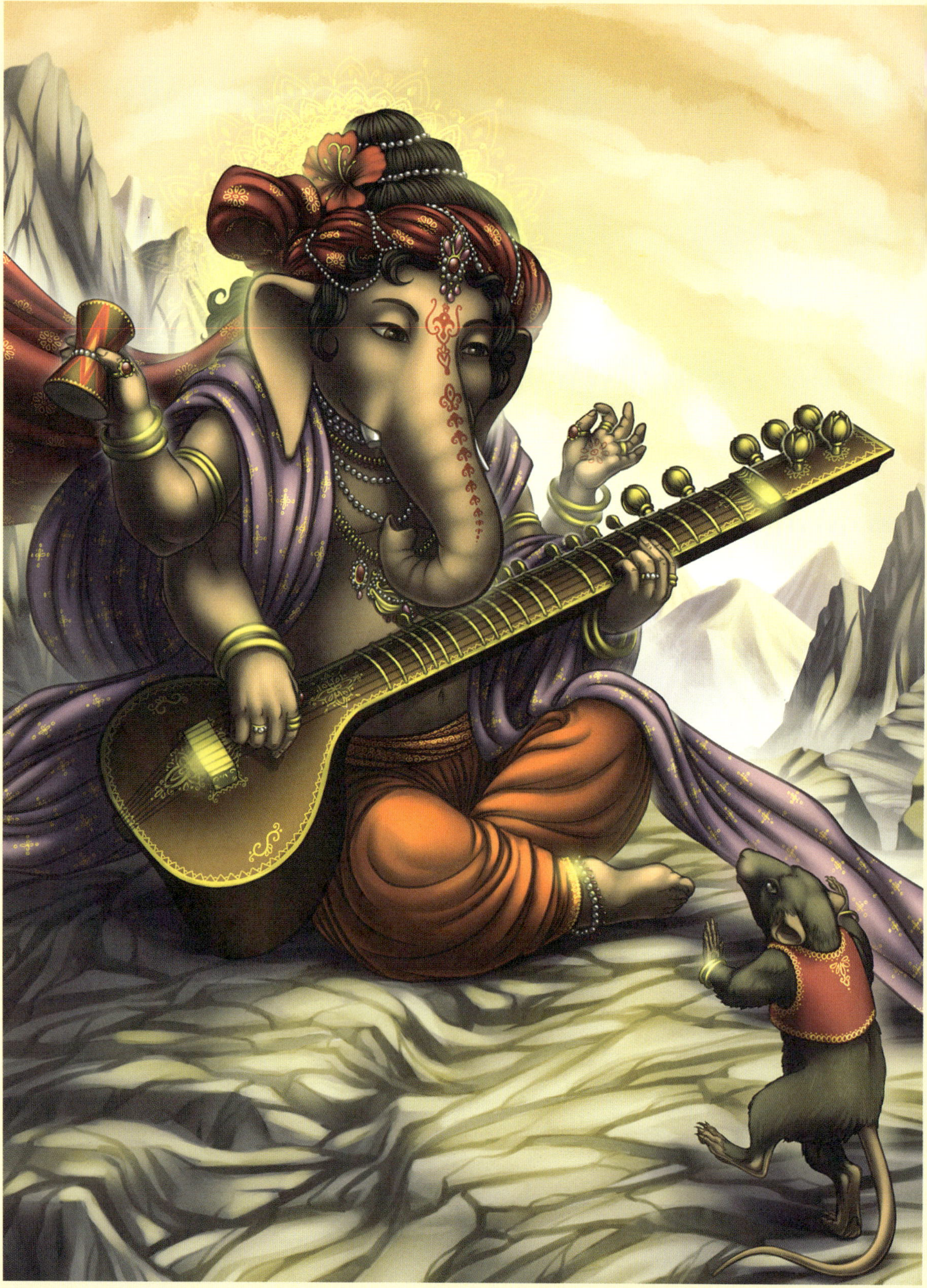

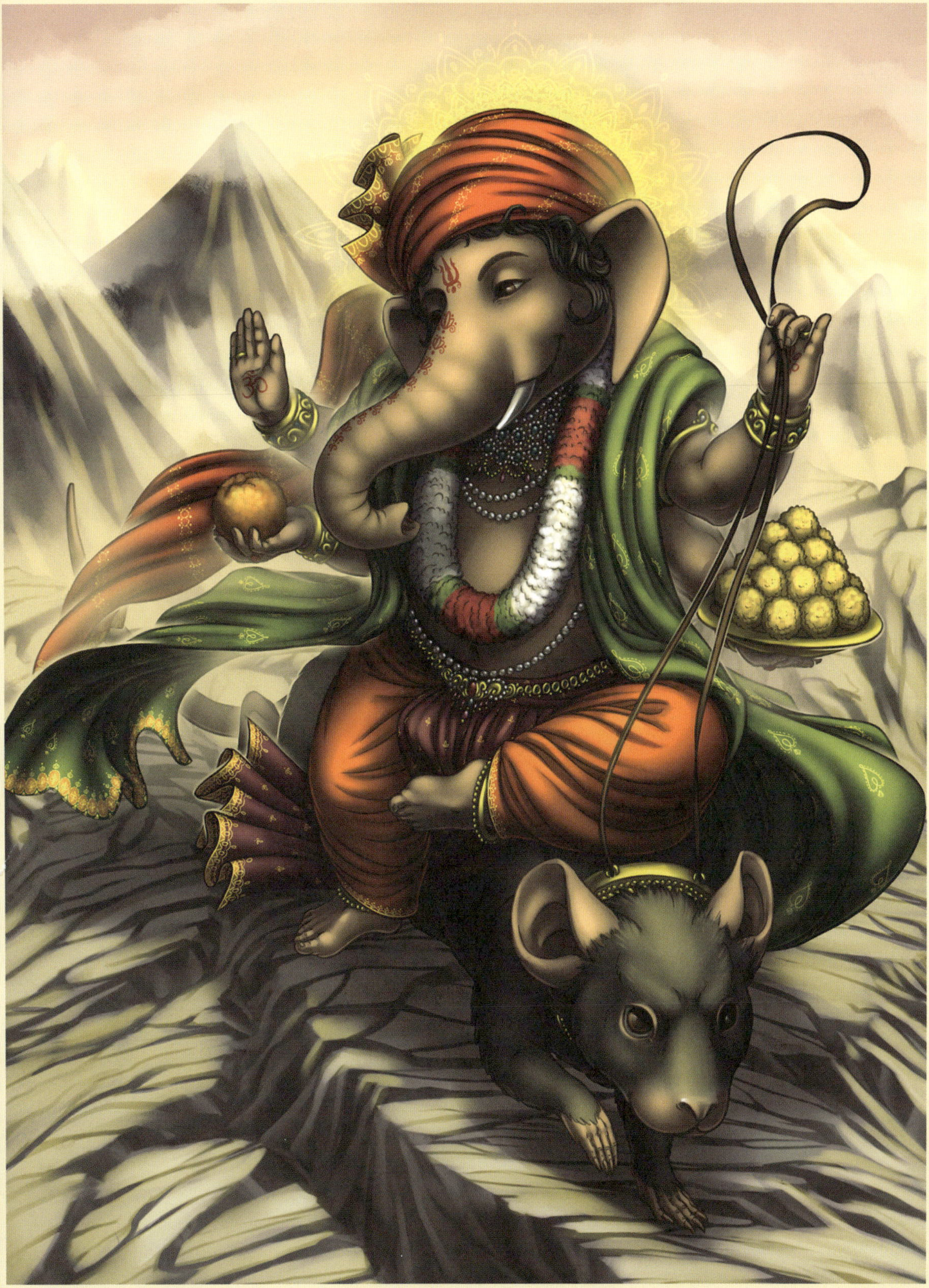

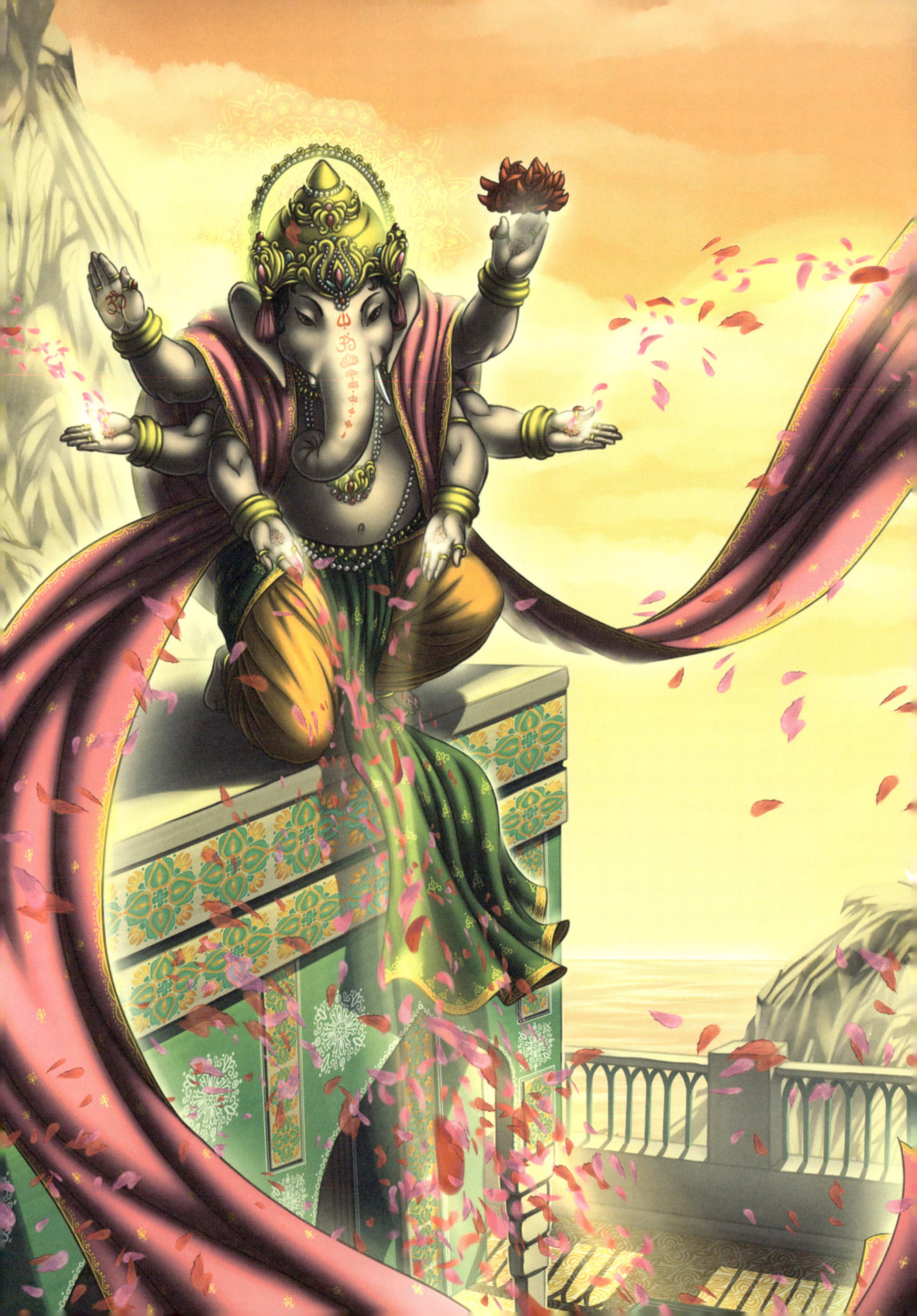

*Call on Ganesha every day – for guidance, to renew your mind
and to refresh your thinking.*

Ganesha blesses you with luck, love and new prospects.

Ganesha is working to clear the obstacles and amp up your blessings.

Ganesha teaches that your blessings are continuous.

You are responsible for creating and generating your success.

*Ganesha asks you to work on integrating and accepting the
spiritual truth that you create your own reality.*

> *Don't let life's challenges discourage you. Some things are just out of your control. Make it work for you! The most painful lessons of the past can teach you how to survive in the present.*
> — Carlos Wallace

Awaken to what you are surrounding yourself with at this moment.

'Om Gum Ganapataya Namaha' is a powerful Ganesha mantra from Ganapati Upanishad. When chanted repeatedly, it is said to invoke Ganesha to clear obstacles from your path. Try it!

Ganesha urges you to let beauty penetrate your heart.

If your critical voice has been overactive or you have been dwelling on negative behaviors, take a moment to realign yourself.

Joy happens when the heart and the soul unite.

*It is important to realize that you came into this lifetime to undergo
certain experiences and to learn very specific life lessons.*

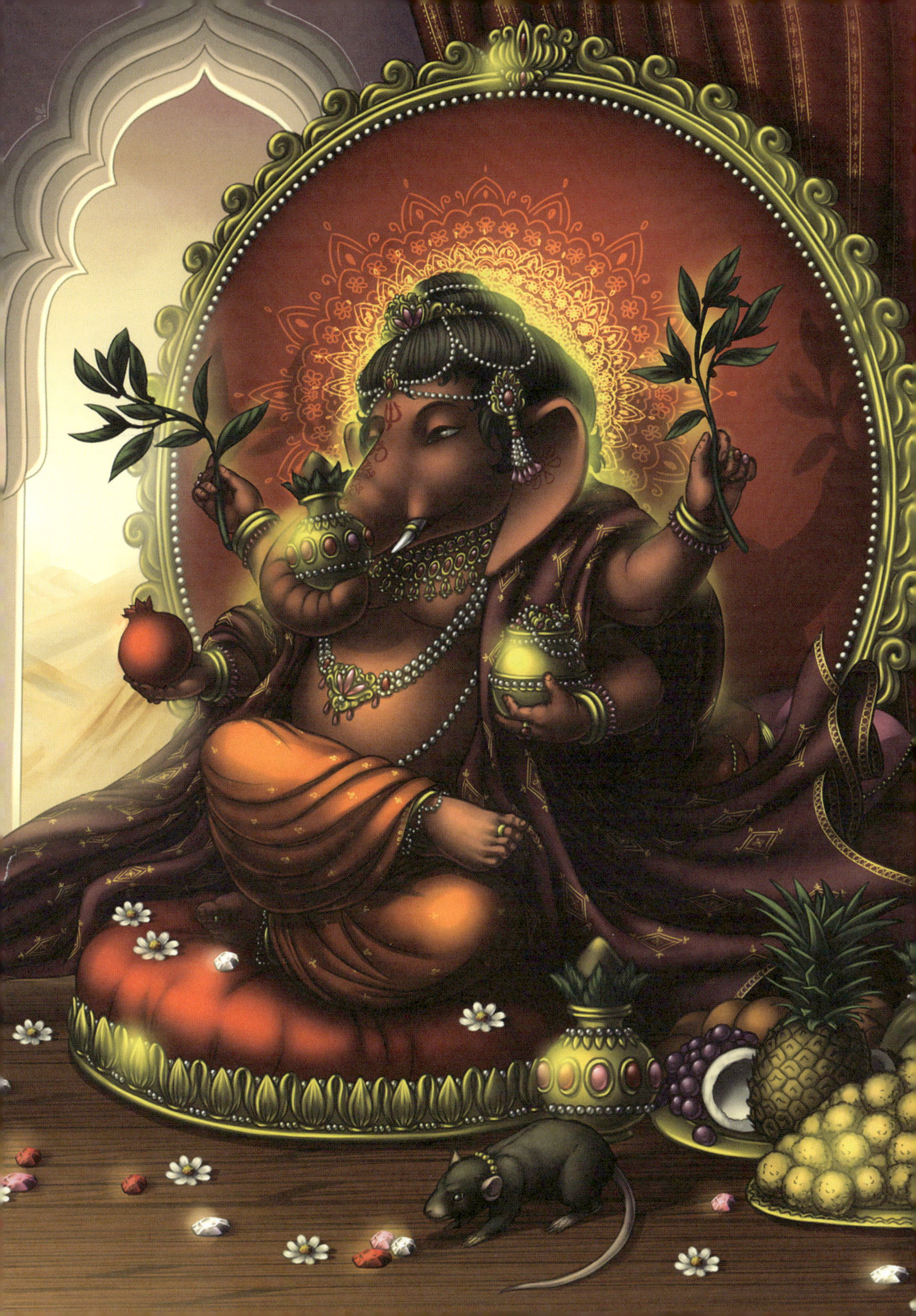

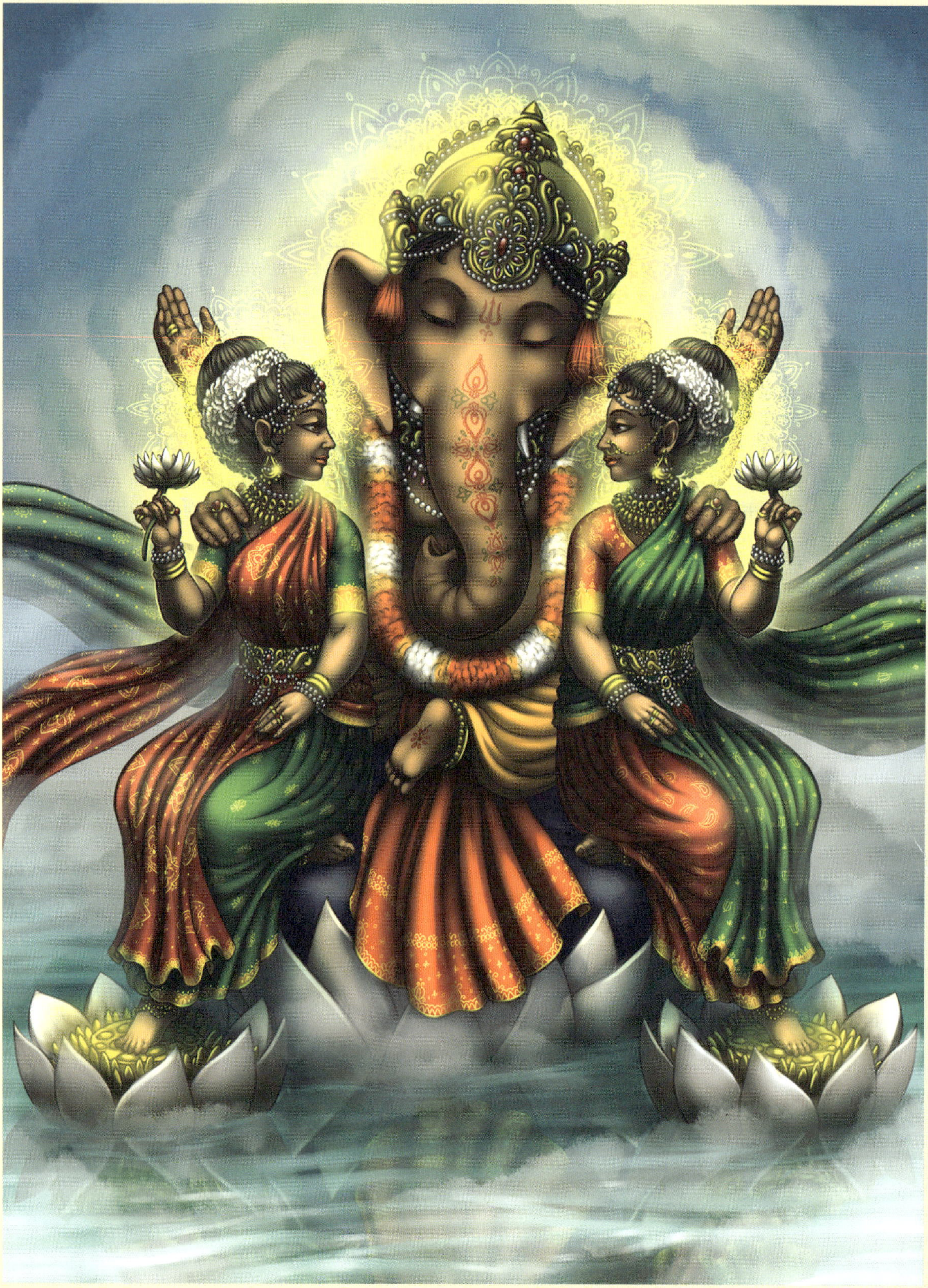

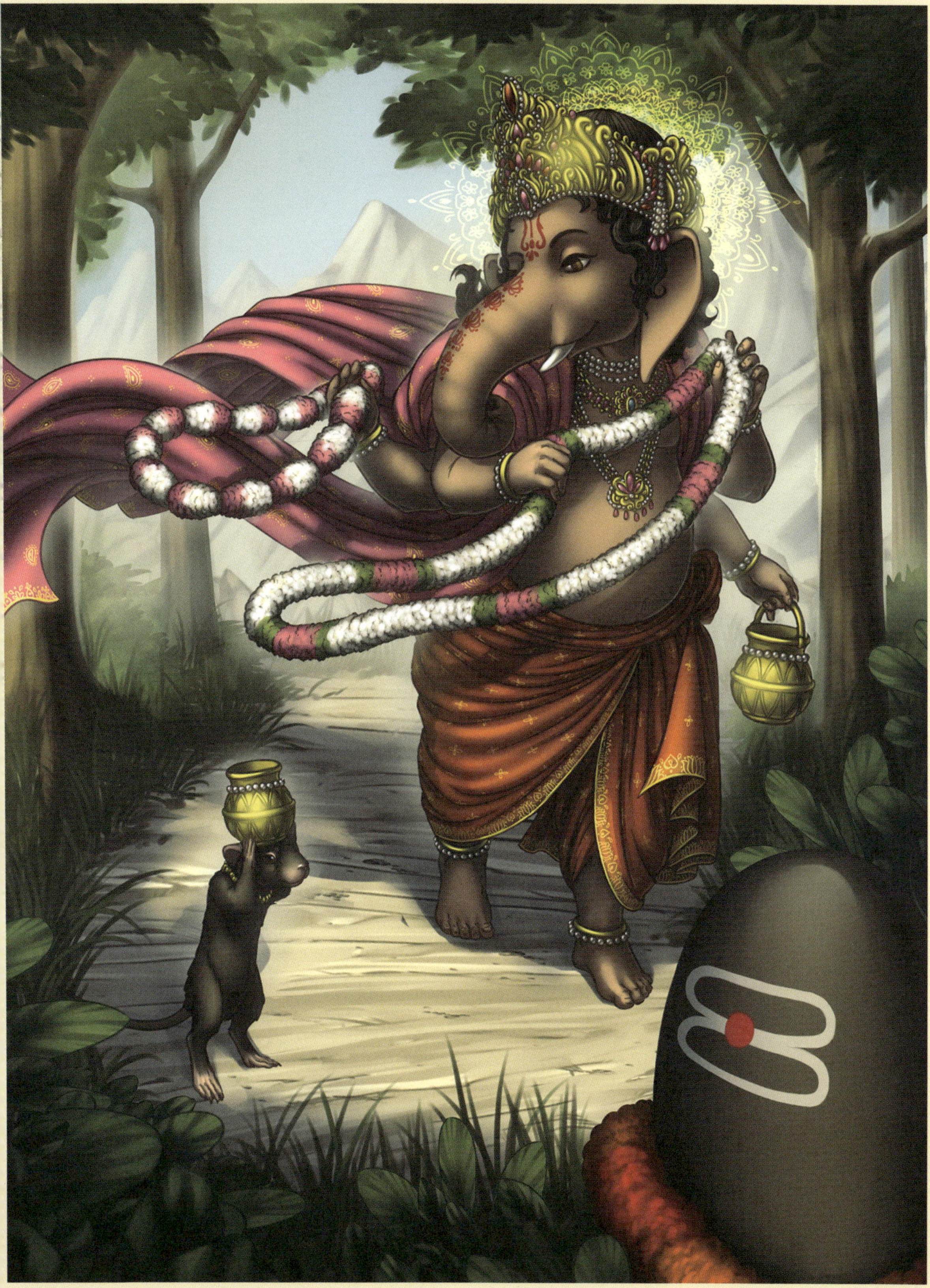

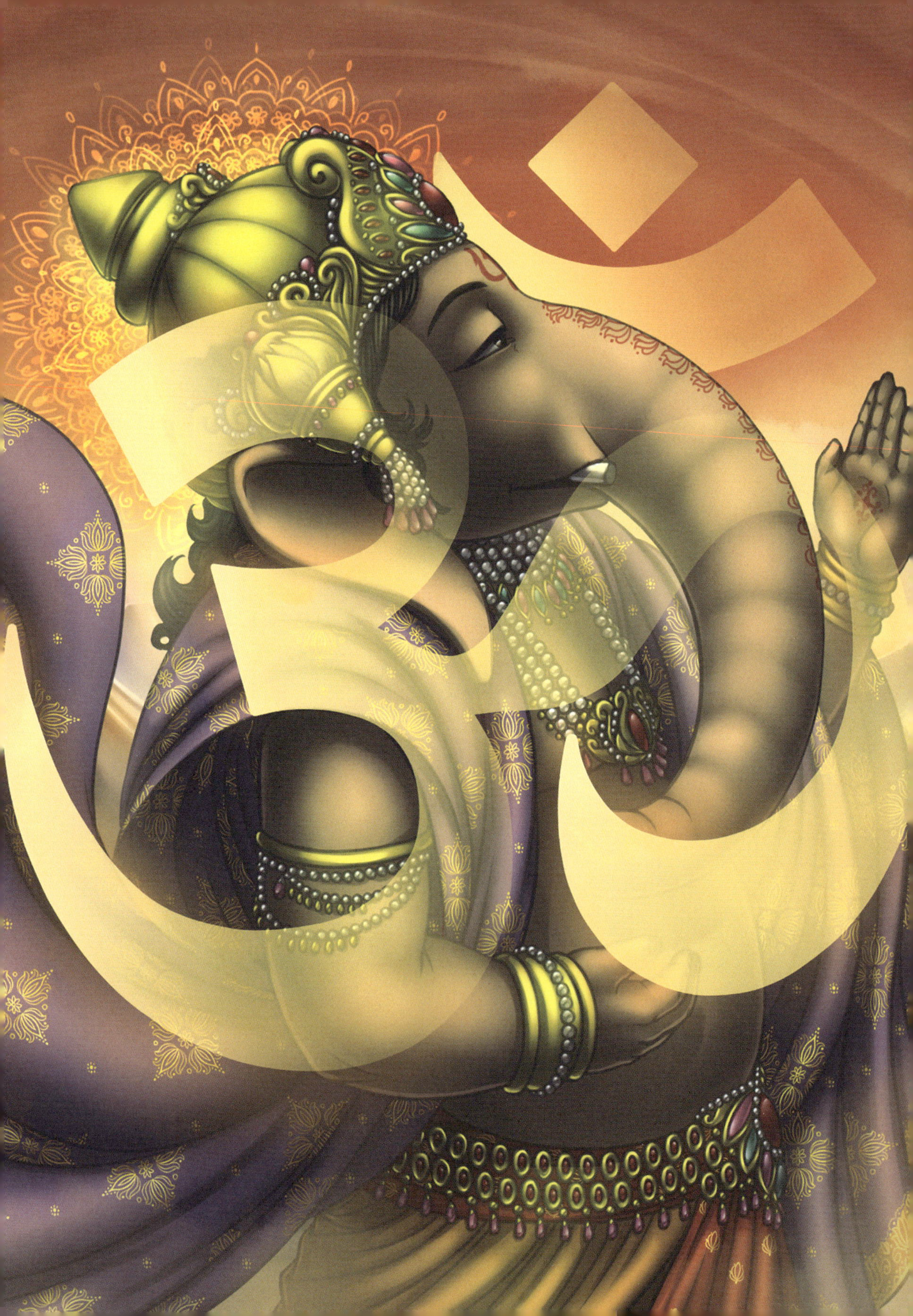

*Share your thoughts, feelings, emotions and anxieties with those who support you.
Better yet, write those thoughts down and then release them.*

Your energy and your inner light are shifting to reveal your life's grand plan.

Ganesha is ready to share his innate wisdom, knowledge and guidance.

Ganesha wants to assist you on your life path.

Knowing yourself is the beginning of all wisdom.
— Aristotle

*Dedicating time to relaxation provides a solid foundation for a
more-balanced, less-stressful life.*

*Affirmations are a great tool to help you relax
and grow in body, mind and spirit.*

*When you have the courage to be true to yourself, you will
feel empowered to act and live in ways true to your own soul,
without any illusion.*

*You are capable of leadership, achievement and inspiring others
through your own success.*

*O, Elephant Faced One!
You are so near and we are far from You.
You are in and we are out;
You are at home, while I'm a stranger.
Yet, You have destroyed my egoity.
I shall sing Your Praise forever
and lay my garland of songs at Your feet.*

— Saint Nambiandiyadigal

Oh divine beings of all three worlds, Let us bring our minds to rest in the darsana of Him who has one tusk. Let us meditate upon Him who has the form of an elephant with a curved trunk. May He guide us always long the right path.
— A Prayer to Lord Ganesha

Ganesha promises great success if you are willing to let down your walls.

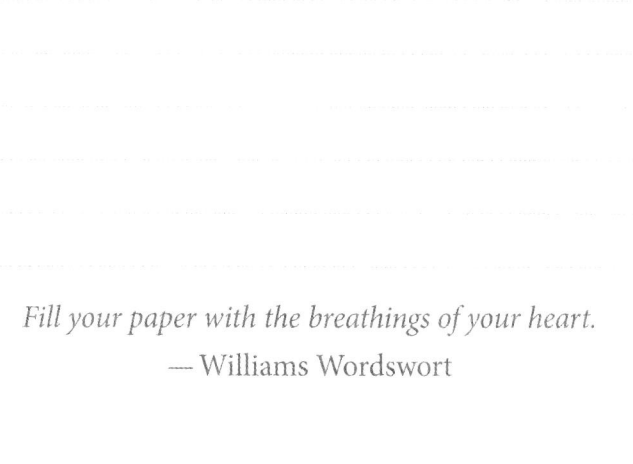

Fill your paper with the breathings of your heart.
— Williams Wordswort

*By His grace beatific, He makes me know my Self. That art nondual,
eternal, real, pure existence, pure consciousness and everlasting bliss.*
— Saint Auvaiyar